Cambridge Elements

Elements in Research Methods for Developmental Science
edited by
Brett Laursen
Florida Atlantic University

NEW APPROACHES TO ASSESSING BEHAVIORAL AND BRAIN SYNCHRONY IN INFANT-PARENT DYADS

Teresa Wilcox
Florida Atlantic University

Jacqueline Stotler Hammack
Florida Atlantic University

Lindsey Riera-Gomez
Florida Atlantic University

Mini Sharma
Ariel University

Hila Gvirts
Ariel University

CAMBRIDGE
UNIVERSITY PRESS

Shaftesbury Road, Cambridge CB2 8EA, United Kingdom

One Liberty Plaza, 20th Floor, New York, NY 10006, USA

477 Williamstown Road, Port Melbourne, VIC 3207, Australia

314–321, 3rd Floor, Plot 3, Splendor Forum, Jasola District Centre,
New Delhi – 110025, India

103 Penang Road, #05–06/07, Visioncrest Commercial, Singapore 238467

Cambridge University Press is part of Cambridge University Press & Assessment,
a department of the University of Cambridge.

We share the University's mission to contribute to society through the pursuit of
education, learning and research at the highest international levels of excellence.

www.cambridge.org
Information on this title: www.cambridge.org/9781009631167

DOI: 10.1017/9781009631174

© Teresa Wilcox, Jacqueline Stotler Hammack, Lindsey Riera-Gomez,
Mini Sharma, and Hila Gvirts 2025

This publication is in copyright. Subject to statutory exception and to the provisions
of relevant collective licensing agreements, no reproduction of any part may take
place without the written permission of Cambridge University Press & Assessment.

When citing this work, please include a reference to the DOI 10.1017/9781009631174

First published 2025

A catalogue record for this publication is available from the British Library

ISBN 978-1-009-63116-7 Hardback
ISBN 978-1-009-63119-8 Paperback
ISSN 2632-9964 (online)
ISSN 2632-9956 (print)

Cambridge University Press & Assessment has no responsibility for the persistence
or accuracy of URLs for external or third-party internet websites referred to in this
publication and does not guarantee that any content on such websites is, or will remain,
accurate or appropriate.

For EU product safety concerns, contact us at Calle de José Abascal, 56, 1°, 28003
Madrid, Spain, or email eugpsr@cambridge.org

New Approaches to Assessing Behavioral and Brain Synchrony in Infant-Parent Dyads

Elements in Research Methods for Developmental Science

DOI: 10.1017/9781009631174
First published online: November 2025

Teresa Wilcox
Florida Atlantic University

Jacqueline Stotler Hammack
Florida Atlantic University

Lindsey Riera-Gomez
Florida Atlantic University

Mini Sharma
Ariel University

Hila Gvirts
Arial University

Author for correspondence: Teresa Wilcox, wilcoxt@fau.edu

Abstract: Historically, infant–parent synchrony has been measured using methods that provide a global assessment of interpersonal synchrony, representing the quality of dyadic interactions. These approaches have illuminated much about synchrony as a broad construct but lack granular details on the temporal dynamics of these interactions. This Element introduces technologically advanced methods for assessing brain and behavior that can offer detailed insights into the dynamic temporal structure of infant–parent social exchanges. These advancements will significantly enhance our understanding of the bidirectional processes that underpin early emerging dyadic exchanges and how these vary across time and context.

Keywords: infant-parent synchrony, hyperscanning, automated coding of behaviour, fNIRS, behavioral synchrony.

© Teresa Wilcox, Jacqueline Stotler Hammack, Lindsey Riera-Gomez, Mini Sharma, and Hila Gvirts 2025

ISBNs: 9781009631167 (HB), 9781009631198 (PB), 9781009631174 (OC)
ISSNs: 2632-9964 (online), 2632-9956 (print)

Contents

1 Introduction   1

2 Behavioral Measures of Interpersonal Synchrony   3

3 Neural Measures of Interpersonal Synchrony   29

4 Interpersonal Synchrony: Coupling of Behavior and Brain   39

5 A New Approach to the Coupling of Brain and Behavior: Phase Patterning and Direction   45

6 Conclusions   59

References   64

1 Introduction

Humans are inherently social beings who rely on affiliation for well-being and survival. Developing well-synchronized interpersonal relations is one way to facilitate social affiliation (Feldman, 2012). Dyadic interpersonal synchrony refers to the dynamic, reciprocal, temporal coordination of actions, thoughts, emotion, and physiology between two partners (Feldman, 2007). Synchronized interactions are built through mutual regulatory, bidirectional processes, where both members of the dyad play a role in shaping the interaction. Achieving dyadic synchrony allows both partners to move flexibly into and between coordinated states. Interpersonal synchrony is observed in infant-parent dyads from the early months of life and plays a key role in developmental outcomes (Feldman et al., 1996; Golds et al., 2022; Kellerman et al., 2020). In later years, interpersonal synchrony is fundamental to effective social exchange, facilitates cooperation, and is an essential component of social-cognitive functioning (Hove & Risen, 2009; Koehne et al., 2016; Valdesolo et al., 2010).

When studying interpersonal synchrony, it is critical for researchers to be clear about the type of synchrony that is under investigation. Dyadic interpersonal synchrony is a complex phenomenon that can be measured in many different ways, including through verbal and nonverbal communicative and emotional behaviors (e.g., talking, pointing, smiling, looking), movement patterns (e.g., direction and speed of motor behaviors), physiological measures (e.g., heart rate, respiration, cortisol, oxytocin), and patterns of neural activation (i.e., typically measured using fNIRS, EEG, MEG, fMRI). The focus of this Element is on methods that assess interpersonal synchrony through verbal and nonverbal behavior, movement patterns, and patterns of cortical activation. For more information on interpersonal synchrony as explored through rhythmic, coordinated physiologic responses, reviews are available (Bell, 2020; DePasquale, 2020; Feldman, 2007).

How one measures interpersonal synchrony is guided by the synchrony-related construct in which one is interested, and the behaviors that best exemplify that construct. Early in the first year, dyadic synchrony is observed in shared emotional states, joint attention, and temporally aligned movement patterns (Nguyen et al., 2020; Piazza et al., 2020). Synchrony is also observed in coordinated brain activity between social partners (Nguyen et al., 2020; Piazza et al., 2020). As social interactions become more varied and diverse during infancy, the manifestation of dyadic synchrony also evolves. These coordinated interactions between infants and their caregivers help infants form attachments, develop social skills, and provide opportunities to share knowledge (Feldman, 2007). Hence, it is critical to that we understand the intricacies of interpersonal synchrony from multiple perspectives. To do so requires a clear understanding of the methods that we use to test our research questions. With advances in technology, the techniques available to researchers to assess interpersonal synchrony in multiple modalities are rapidly changing.

Our overarching goal is to promote methods that allow us to better understand the origins and development of dyadic interpersonal synchrony as a bidirectional process that emerges within the many different contexts in which infants, parents, and caretakers interact. This Element begins by discussing traditional approaches to the assessment of infant-parent synchrony, which rely primarily on person-coded assessments of verbal and nonverbal behavior. Next, we introduce more contemporary approaches that incorporate technologically advanced methods for the automated coding of movement data. We will then discuss hyperscanning, focusing primarily on the use of functional near-infrared spectroscopy (fNIRS). Hyperscanning is a neuroimaging technique that measures neural activity in two or more individuals simultaneously during interactions. Hyperscanning is crucial for uncovering the neural underpinnings of interpersonal synchrony because it captures the dynamic and reciprocal nature of social interactions which cannot be fully understood by a traditional single-brain approach, in which the individual brain is studied in isolation.

We will discuss approaches that incorporate measures of behavior and brain simultaneously, using the relation between behavioral responses, movement patterns, and patterns of neural activation to understand the complex unfolding of dyadic interactions during social exchange. These interactional patterns can be measured in a number of dimensions, including when they occur, the strength with which they occur, the frequency with which they occur, and the phase in which they occur (e.g., who leads and who follows). Within this context, we will introduce a new method for analyzing signals obtained from behavioral and neural assessments that can provide more detailed information about the coordinated, dynamic temporal structure of infant-parent dyadic interactions. This method allows us to uncover the different types of interactions that occur between parents and their infants during different tasks. Together, these advancements will shed light on the processes that support early emerging social interactions and possible mechanisms for change in the quality and quantity of these interpersonal exchanges.

Our focus is primarily on infancy and toddlerhood (i.e., 3 months of age to 3 years of age). However, there are sections of this Element where the literature with this age group is sparse. Hence, we will turn to investigatory methods and data analytic techniques implemented in early childhood (i.e., 3 years of age to 6 years of age), and with older children and adults to explain why it is advantageous for developmental scientists to consider these alternatives.

Finally, most infant research investigating interpersonal synchrony has been conducted with infant-mother dyads, largely because mothers are more accessible research participants than fathers or other caregivers. In studies that have included fathers, some, but not all, have reported differences in the way that mothers and fathers temporally coordinate with their infants (Azhari, Bizzego, & Esposito, 2022; Feldman, 2007; Liu, Zhu et al., 2024; Lundy, 2023; Nguyen, Schleihauf, Kungl et al., 2021). The extent to which mothers and fathers differ in their dyadic interactions with their infants depends, at least in part, on how synchrony is measured and the context in which it is measured. We will be explicit when reporting findings from studies that included both mothers and fathers and in which gender differences were obtained.

2 Behavioral Measures of Interpersonal Synchrony

There is a long-standing interest in the developmental sciences in identifying the ways in which coordinated social interactions in infant-parent dyads are established and maintained. In this section, we first present person-coded measures of interpersonal synchrony, which have been used for many years in the assessment of infant-mother interactions. Person-coded assessments, which evaluate a broad range of verbal and nonverbal communicative and emotional behaviors, are frequently taken during spontaneous, unstructured play. This play context enables researchers to observe infant-parent interactions during a context that closely mirrors their everyday experiences. However, assessment can be done in more structured settings.

We then present more contemporary automated approaches to assessing behavioral interactions that include (a) wearable technology, which typically requires the use of specialized equipment in a lab setting, and (b) automatic coding of behavior, which utilizes computational methods to estimate synchronous behaviors in a video stream and is more flexible in the situations in which can be used.

2.1 Person-coded Measures

The most widely used behavioral assessments for evaluating interpersonal synchrony in infant-parent dyads rely on trained observers to code various aspects of verbal and nonverbal behavior during a dyadic interaction (see Table 1). These behaviors, often subtle and complex, are assigned numerical values that are averaged to produce composite or global scores reflecting the overall quality of the interaction. Person-coded measures typically include monadic global scores, which assess the behaviors of the infant or parent individually (e.g., infant engagement or parental sensitivity), as well as dyadic

Table 1 Person-coded assessments of interpersonal synchrony

Type and Description	Advantages	Limitations	Types of Research Questions
Global coding scales assess infant behaviors, parent behaviors, and dyadic coordination. Composite scores capture monadic constructs (e.g., maternal sensitivity, infant initiative) and dyadic constructs (e.g., dyadic reciprocity).	Well-established coding schemes with good psychometric properties are available. Verbal and nonverbal behaviors are considered. Composite scores can be used as predictor or outcome variables.	Time and resource intensive and susceptible to observer bias. Scores do not capture moment-to-moment changes in dyadic interactions.	How do monadic traits influence dyadic interactions? How do monadic and dyadic traits relate to developmental outcomes? How do interpersonal constructs measured through behavioral coding align with those assessed through other modalities? To what extent are individual and dyadic characteristics causes or consequences of other variables (e.g., emotion regulation, attachment)?
Micro-coding of infant and parent behaviors includes frame-by-frame analysis. The onset, offset, duration, and frequency of synchrony-related behaviors are coded.	Captures moment-to-moment changes in monadic and dyadic behaviors.	Time and resource intensive and susceptible to observer bias.	How do specific behaviors or classes of behaviors influence dyadic synchrony? How are synchrony-related behaviors related to developmental outcomes (e.g., language development or communicative behaviors)? What is the relation between the timing or onset of specific behaviors and that of neural synchrony?

Note: Person-coded measures are applied to a previously acquired video stream.

global scores, which evaluate the quality of the interaction between the two (e.g., dyadic reciprocity or mutual adaptation).

Person-coded measures of interpersonal synchrony are most often implemented by using a video-recorded session of the infant-parent interaction, which is then later coded offline. Projects that implement person-coded measures typically use video recordings from a 4- to 11-minute naturalistic free play task, although video recordings are sometimes obtained from tasks that are more structured (such as periods of interaction during feeding, bedtime, bath time), or during tasks of a direct experimental instruction (such as still-face procedures) (Leclère et al., 2014). We recommend using person-coded assessments during naturalistic free play interaction when the research question pertains to spontaneous dyadic infant-parent behaviors that occur during normal day-to-day interactions. Study designs that incorporate a naturalistic free play interaction may maintain more ecological validity and the behavioral findings may be more generalizable than would be for some structured research designs. If the research question is dependent on the study of a specific behavior (such as index-finger pointing) or situation (such as building a block tower), we recommend that the researcher implement person-coded assessments of behavior in a more structured study design to ensure that specific behavior or scenario of interest is present in the data.

Person-coded behavioral assessments that generate global scores are well-suited for statistical analyses that require a single score, or small set of scores, to represent the quality of infant-parent synchrony during the entire social interaction. Some behavioral methods include options for micro-coding, which provide detailed scores for specific behaviors observed over brief, targeted time intervals. Although definitions of synchrony may vary across disciplines and theoretical perspectives, within the developmental sciences synchrony is typically characterized by mutuality or reciprocity between partners, rhythmic and harmonious exchanges, and sustained engagement (for a review, see Leclère et al., 2014). Finally, though interpersonal synchrony is related to constructs such as parent sensitivity, interpersonal synchrony is a distinct construct that highlights temporal aspects of dynamic social interaction.

2.1.1 Implementation of Person-coded Measures

The investigator should consider their research question and study design (naturalistic vs. structured) when considering how best to record video data of the experiment and implement the person-coded measures. Best practices for offline coding of parent-infant synchrony include (but are not limited to) the coder's ability to clearly see the parent's and infant's facial expressions, hand gestures, and any objects of joint attention (such as toys), as well as the coder's ability to clearly understand the parent's words and the infant's vocalizations. To achieve the goal of full visibility, we recommend using multiple cameras positioned at different angles. For example, it may be beneficial to have cameras positioned to directly face the parent, the infant, and the dyad as a whole, as well as having an overhead camera that is positioned to obtain a view of the dyad's hands and objects of interest.

For research studies that require participants to attend to an object of joint attention, we advise that the participants be seated at a tabletop across from one another, allowing for ease of communication and joint involvement with the object. However, parents may be more comfortable playing on the floor than at a table. Choice of seating arrangement and toys/objects used during the session needs to be developmentally appropriate. For example, prior to about 7 months infants are unable to sit unsupported, hence will require trunk support to have their hands free during the task. Once infants gain the ability to sit independently, their reaching and object manipulation abilities improve (Bertenthal & Clifton, 1998; Rochat & Goubet, 1995; Soska et al., 2010), leading to greater mobility and object exploration skills. In comparison, older infants will not need sitting support but may benefit from an arrangement that keeps them in a location within camera view.

To increase ecological validity, researchers may choose to collect data in the home of the participants rather than in the laboratory setting. This can be done by bringing all necessary data collection tools (such as cameras, tripods, and any specific toys or objects needed) to the participant's home. The experimenter may also allow the participants to interact with any of their own toys or household items as they choose, rather than experimenter-chosen toys and objects, as the presence of familiar items may provide a more accurate picture of how the dyad interacts during their daily routines. Our team has had success collecting free play data from a home setting using online video conferencing software (Hammack et al., 2023). This method reduces the resources needed, maintains a naturalistic play setting, and increases the ecological validity of the experimental findings, as compared to researchers traveling to the participants' home. There are some disadvantages of online video data collection techniques, including attrition due to interruptions from other children or family members, technical or internet problems, bad lighting, noisy environments, or procedural problems (e.g., lack of a tabletop appropriately distanced from a camera). However, the advantages of online video data collection, including increased accessibility to a larger and more diverse group of participants in their natural environment, may outweigh the limitations of online video data collection.

2.1.2 Global Coding of Dyadic Qualities

By using a global coding approach, nuances in behavior can be evaluated by experienced coders, who evaluate a range of behaviors to obtain a global measure of dyadic constructs assessed across the entirety of the interaction. Global coding is well suited for the measurement of concepts such as reciprocity or mutuality and reflects the overall quality of the interaction within the scoring paradigm. This approach requires the coder to consider the wide context of the interaction when rating behaviors, which allows the investigator insights into the infant-parent relationship that would not be possible through means of self-report or the observation of the infant behavior alone.

Studies that use a dyadic approach to the study of infant-parent synchrony can provide information about the dyadic relationship that cannot be deduced from the coding of infant and parent behaviors individually. For example, mutually responsive orientation is an established dyadic construct that cannot be measured by assessing responsiveness and positive affect of each social partner individually (Aksan et al., 2006). Next, we will review popular measures that include dyadic constructs for the investigation of parent-child interactions.

Measures of Reciprocity. One well-validated global coding measure, the Coding Interactive Behavior scale (CIB; Feldman, 1998), uses a rating system to assess dyadic reciprocity and dyadic negative states. In the CIB, dyadic reciprocity indexes the degree of reciprocal turn-taking, adaptation to one another's emotional states and levels of interest and activity, and fluency of the interaction. A global score of dyadic reciprocity is calculated as an average score of three dyadic codes: dyadic reciprocity, dyadic adaptation-regulation, and dyadic fluency. The dyadic negative states measure is calculated as an average of two dyadic codes: dyadic constriction and dyadic tension. Other global coding measures, such as the Qualitative Ratings for Parent-Child Interaction scale (Owen et al., 1996), the Coding System for Mother-Child Interactions (CMSCI; Healey et al., 2010), and the NCAT Feeding and Teaching PCI scales (Keefe et al., 1996) assess similar dyadic constructs within the context of infant-parent interactions.

Measures of Synchrony. Other global coding techniques consider child-parent synchronous behaviors, whether it is the coder's perception of synchronous behaviors during interaction or the treatment of synchrony as a more global concept without measure of the temporal dynamics (see Leclère et al., 2014 for a review of coding techniques of infant-parent synchrony). The Bernieri's Scale (Bernieri et al., 1988), The Belsky Parent-Child Interaction Coding System (Isabella & Belsky, 1991), and the Synchrony Global Coding System (Skuban et al., 2006) measure the coder's perception of synchronous behaviors during interaction. The Coding Scheme and The Rocissano and Yatchmink Taxonomy require the coder to separate the interaction videos into several parts and rate overall synchrony across each part of the session. The Maternal-Infant Synchrony Scale assesses engagement during feeding interactions (Reyna et al., 2012). Similarly, the Rating Scale of Interactional Style (RSIS; Feldman et al., 1996), the Infant Caregiver Engagement (ICE) scale (Weinberg et al., 1999), and the Behavior State Coding Scale (Field et al., 1989) assess mutual synchrony as a global construct.

Measures of Mutuality. Some common global measures of dyadic infant-parent behaviors include measures of mutuality, which describe the "cooperative, smooth-flowing, and responsive nature of a parent and child engaging together" (see Funamoto & Rinaldi, 2015, for a review of child-parent mutuality coding schemes). Such measures of mutuality include The Parent-Child Interaction System (PARCHISY; Deater-Deckard et al., 1997), The Mutually Responsive Orientation Scale (MRO; Aksan et al., 2006), The Caregiver-Child Affect, Responsiveness, and Engagement Scale (C-CARES; Tamis-LeMonda et al., 2002), and the Synchrony and Control Coding Scheme (Mize & Pettit, 1997). These coding schemes cover several dyadic behaviors including communication, reciprocity, and coordination.

Studies that use a global approach to investigate infant-parent synchrony reveal a great deal about the factors that impact the early dynamic social relationship developing between infants and their parents (see Golds et al., 2022 for a review). For example, parental warmth and sensitivity is associated with higher levels of synchrony (Longhi, 2009; Thompson & Trevathan, 2009). Global approaches have also demonstrated that maternal mental health risk factors, such as depressive symptoms (Coburn et al., 2015; Field et al., 1989), emotion dysregulation (Lotzin et al., 2015), anxiety (Lemus et al., 2022; Moore et al., 2016), and maternal stress (Coburn et al., 2015; Lemus et al., 2022) are associated with lower levels of infant-parent synchrony. Additionally, studies using a global-coding approach have demonstrated the lasting impact that early-emerging infant-parent dyadic synchrony has on developmental outcomes. For example, greater interpersonal synchrony in the first year is associated with better expressive and receptive language skills (Kellerman et al., 2020), more symbolic play, and enhanced performance on intelligence tests years later (Feldman et al., 1996; Feldman & Greenbaum, 1997). In the social domain, studies using globally coded measures of infant-parent and toddler-parent synchrony demonstrate that synchrony is positively associated with better child self-regulation skills (see Davis et al., 2017 for a meta-analysis on the topic), and globally rated child-parent synchrony is predictive of child social skills and aggression in preschool-aged children (see Pasiak & Menna, 2015 for a review).

2.1.3 Micro-Coding of Interpersonal Synchrony

Micro-coding approaches are coding paradigms that allow trained coders to evaluate instances of infant and parent behaviors during specific timepoints during the interaction. By analyzing the time series of behavior from both social partners, researchers have the ability to investigate the temporal dynamics of infant-parent synchrony (i.e., how infant-parent synchrony changes throughout the course of an interaction). The paradigm may require the coder to identify both infant and parent instances independently, or instead to identify joint behaviors exhibited by both partners in the dyad (de Graag et al., 2012; Isabella et al., 1989). From either approach, a measure of interpersonal behavioral synchrony can be obtained by extracting simultaneous, sequential, or lagged behaviors (Feldman, 2007) that occur within the dyadic interaction during a specified time frame. Synchrony can be observed across many different behaviors. For example, researchers may choose to micro-code instances of joint attention, affective states, vocalizations, or nonverbal communications (Bizzego et al., 2022; Nguyen, Abney et al., 2021; Papoutselou et al., 2024; Piazza et al., 2020). In fact, synchrony among caregiver-child interactions often involves the coordination of intermodal behaviors. For example, mother-initiated acts may often involve verbal language paired with instances of child positive affect and gaze to mother. Distinct from constructs of imitation and mimicry, infant-parent synchrony is thought of as an "intricate dance" between social partners (Feldman, 2007) which can be operationalized through statistical analysis of the micro-coded time series (see Leclère et al., 2014 for a review of micro-coding approaches to study infant-parent synchrony).

Micro-coding of infant-parent synchronous behaviors is sometimes conducted on a frame-by-frame basis, meaning that the coder investigates behaviors on each frame in the video to identify specific onsets and offsets of behaviors as they occur. Sometimes researchers code behaviors in windows as narrow as 0.01 second frames (Atzil et al., 2014), or in windows as broad as three-second intervals (Doba et al., 2022). Although very narrow windows can increase the temporal resolution of the collected data, this may also increase the coding workload. The expected duration of the behavior of interest to the research question will determine the interval used. When micro-coding frame-by-frame, typically onsets are marked in the frame in which the specified behavior begins, and offsets are marked in the frame in which the specified behavior ends (Kellerman et al., 2020). Computerized coding systems, such as Noldus (Wageningen, the Netherlands) and Datavyu (Datavyu Team, 2014), can be used to assist in frame-by-frame micro-coding (e.g., Atzil et al., 2014; Feldman et al., 2011; Harel et al., 2010; Hoch et al., 2021).

Micro-coding approaches often result in frequency count scores for specific infant and maternal behaviors, sometimes paired with assessment of proportions, mean durations, latencies of time, and may include contingencies with other behaviors (Gordon & Feldman, 2008; Gordon et al., 2010; Kellerman et al., 2020). The Monadic Phase Manual has been used to cross-correlate infant and mother time series to assess bidirectional influences of dyadic moment-to-moment behaviors (Tronick & Cohn, 1989). Other approaches to micro-coding synchrony include assessment of second-by-second correlation of behaviors (Ham & Tronick, 2009; Karger, 1979; Moore & Calkins, 2004;), assessment of positive lead-lags between two corresponding time series (Feldman, 2003), or assessment of mean duration of synchronous behaviors (Atzil et al., 2014; Gratier, 2003).

Researchers have chosen different modalities of behavior to investigate as indicators for synchrony when using a micro-coding approach to study of infant-parent synchrony. For example, researchers have micro-coded instances of gaze synchrony, affect synchrony, vocalization and speech synchrony, touch synchrony, motor synchrony, and proximity synchrony (Atzil et al., 2014; Doba et al., 2022; Feldman et al., 2011; Kellerman et al., 2020).

One can also consider more than one modality of behavior when calculating a score for infant-parent synchrony. Considering various modalities of behavior in one synchrony measure allows for the capture of instances in which one partner initiates a synchronous moment in one modality of behavior, and the other partner responds in a different modality of behavior. For example, synchrony can be calculated by coding instances in which mothers coordinated their social gaze and affectionate touch with instances of infant social gaze, positive affect, and vocalizations (Atzil et al., 2014). As another example, a different target behavior such as "look to face" can be used to assess the extent to which target behaviors such as mother vocalizations were responded to by the infant within three seconds (Kellerman et al., 2020).

It is common for a subset of the data, ranging from 10% to 25% (Atzil et al., 2014; Doba et al., 2022; Feldman et al., 2011), to be micro-coded by two independent coders for reliability purposes when implementing micro-coding approaches. One may also consider reporting Cohen's kappa values for inter-rater reliability. Kappa values reported in the literature range from 0.77 (Doba et al., 2022) to 0.99 (Doba et al., 2022), which indicate substantial agreement. Inter-rater reliability can also be reported with an intraclass-correlation coefficient (ICC), with values in the literature reported over 0.70 and averaging 0.88 (Kellerman et al., 2020).

In summary, micro-coding offers a more detailed and nuanced window into the temporal patterns and complexities of infant-parent dyadic interactions. Examples of how micro-coding can be used to investigate research questions about the infant-parent relationship, particularly in conjunction with hyperscanning data, are found in Section 4.2.

2.1.4 Limitations of Person-coded Measures

There are some notable limitations one must consider when using person-coded measures to assess dyadic characteristics of the infant-parent interaction. First, behavioral coding is an extremely laborious and resource intensive process, requiring several hours to code relatively short video interactions. Additionally, a certain degree of subjectivity is inevitably introduced in the coding process. To minimize the influence of coder biases, behavioral coding techniques are often supplemented with detailed manuals defining the scoring of observable behavior. Coders may also be required to engage in extensive training processes to ensure high levels of inter-rater reliability. Although global coding techniques may only require a numeric rating to be assigned when ranking behaviors observed during a social interaction, we advise that coders take detailed notes when coding and refer to corresponding timepoints to justify the score given. This method helps to mediate disagreements between coders, maintain high levels of consistency between sessions, and maintain high levels of reliability between coders. Another limitation of global person-coded measures in particular is that they often lack the temporal information necessary for investigating dynamic moment-by-moment changes over the course of the interaction.

Although micro-coding techniques can mitigate this issue somewhat and offer valuable temporal insights into infant-parent interactions, their subjective nature necessitates the integration of additional objective, quantitative measures of synchrony to fully capture the complex dynamics within this dyadic exchange. Although definitions for interpersonal synchrony often encompass coordination across lags in time (such as when one partner initiates behavior and the social partner responds with another target behavior only moments after), a meta-analysis on infant-parent synchrony determined that only 24–35% of the relevant research articles defined lag or non-constrained lag (Provenzi et al., 2018).

Currently, most studies in the developmental sciences have relied almost exclusively on person-coded scoring systems. Thus, what the field is lacking are objective, automated quantitative behavioral measures that provide information about the temporal dynamics of infant-parent interactions and how this varies across the course of an interaction and by context. One reason for this gap in knowledge is that researchers in the developmental sciences have lacked measurement tools necessary to automatically detect and quantify unique dyadic interaction patterns. In the next section, we demonstrate how these "automatic" tools, originally developed for use with adults, can be applied to quantitatively characterize the complex nature of infant-parent interaction patterns and to systematically explore adaptations of the temporal structure of interactive behaviors during infant-parent exchanges.

2.2 Automated Coding of Behavior

Due to the labor-intensive nature of person-coded methods of synchronization (Pouw et al., 2020), the field has gradually been moving toward more technologically driven, automated methods of synchrony measurement. There are two main approaches. One approach involves the use of wearable technology and the other depends on marker-less computational assessments (see Table 2).

2.2.1 Assessment of Movement Synchrony Using Wearable Technology

There are a wide range of modalities through which interpersonal synchronization between infant-mother dyads can be assessed automatically by using wearable sensors. Of particular interest in this section is movement synchronization. Movement synchronization (sometimes referred to as interpersonal coordination, joint action (Cuadros et al., 2021), interactional synchronization (Dunbar et al., 2022) or nonverbal synchrony (Ramseyer & Tschacher, 2011) is an optimal choice for automated assessment, both due to its ability to be captured with relative ease and its ubiquitous nature. Movement synchronization encapsulates movement matching, mirroring, and the "rhythmic coordination of behavioral patterns" (p. 204, Dunbar et al., 2022), such that it captures both the behavior (movement) and the temporal structures that describe the interrelatedness of said behaviors.

Wearable sensors offer valuable insight into movement synchrony between infant and mother during a variety of social contexts. Several types of wearable sensors are available and have successfully been used with infants to measure both individual body movements and interpersonal, coordinated motion. For example, wearable "smart jumpsuit" that contains several combination accelerometer/gyroscope sensors at key locations can measure the infant's posture and motor movements, including inter-limb synchronization (Airaksinen et al., 2020; Airaksinen et al., 2022). Other wearables include inertial sensors (Franchak et al., 2024), which can be used to record long-form recordings of infant body positioning, and actigraphs (Tsai et al., 2011), a type of accelerometer that measures the speed and degree of body movement. Actigraphy can be used to investigate maternal-infant circadian system synchronization, which are representative of sleep-wake cycles (Tsai et al., 2011). Actigraphs are small, noninvasive devices that can be worn on the wrist or ankle. Associations were

Table 2 Computational approaches to assessing interpersonal synchrony in infant-parent dyads

Type and description	Advantages	Limitations	Types of research questions
Wearable technology applied to user specified body parts. Movement synchrony calculated for specific body parts or groups of body parts.	Allows for fine-grained analysis of coordinated body part movements.	Expensive, specialized equipment required. Technologically challenging to implement. Infants may not tolerate. Lab setting typically required.	How does the coordination among different body parts across partners contribute to dyadic synchrony or interaction quality? How does the coordination of specific body parts across partners contribute to broader dyadic constructs such as mutual engagement or affective attunement? What is the relation between coordinated movement patterns in infant-parent dyads and the engagement of cognitive or social processes in infancy? How are early coordinated movement patterns between infant and parent related to later cognitive, social, or communicative development?

Table 2 (cont.)

Type and description	Advantages	Limitations	Types of research questions
Frame differencing techniques (e.g., motion energy analysis) are applied to user defined regions of interest (i.e., dyad 1 and dyad 2). Total-body movement within the region for each frame is calculated. Movement synchrony between two regions of interest is computed.	Allows for fine-grained movement analysis between regions of interest. Open-source software available. Specialized hardware not required.	Susceptible to data loss for several reasons (e.g., unstable lighting, video quality, overlapping regions of interest). Technologically challenging to implement. Unable to assess coordinated movement in individual body parts.	How do coordinated movement patterns between infant and parent relate to dyadic constructs such as synchrony, reciprocity, or mutual engagement? Do coordinated movement patterns in infant-parent dyads reflect engagement in specific cognitive or social processes? What is the relation between movement synchrony and synchrony assessed in other modalities?
Computer vision techniques (e.g., pose estimation methods) use machine learning algorithms to identify key points on body and track	Allows for fine-grained movement analysis of specific body parts. Open-source software available. Specialized hardware not	Technologically challenging to implement. Machine learning algorithms are different for different sized bodies, hence requires selective adaptation	How does the coordination among different body parts across partners contribute to dyadic synchrony or interaction quality? How does

body part movement across frames. Movement synchrony calculated for specific body parts or groups of body parts.	required. Allows flexibility in selecting body parts of interest for infant and adult participants.	the coordination of specific body parts across partners contribute to broader dyadic constructs? What is the relation between coordinated movement patterns in infant-parent dyads and engagement in specific cognitive or social processes? How are early coordinated movement patterns in infant-parent dyads related to later cognitive, social, or communicative development?

Note: Automated-coding tools generate time-series data.

identified between maternal and infant rhythms, of both activity and circadian patterns, even accounting for data attrition; 37.8% of infant activity data was excluded because the movement being experienced was not generated by the infant independently, as indicated by a parent diary (i.e., riding in a swing or a stroller, being held and swayed, etc.) (Tsai et al., 2011). Thus, wearable sensors are capable of being employed in at-home settings with minimal supervision, as opposed to requiring more structured lab settings, though they may be subject to large amounts of "unknown" movement that may be misreported due to human error.

Several groups have had marked success employing optoelectronic wearables with infants as young as 4 months in more controlled laboratory-based settings (Cuadros et al., 2019; Egmose et al., 2017; Cuadros et al., 2020). In these setups, infants wear bodysuits and hats that can be embedded with reflective infrared markers at the head, wrists, elbows, upper back, and shoulders. Adults wear identical markers, attached to their clothes using Velcro. A specialized infrared camera system then locates the markers and tracks them through three-dimensional space, providing the user with a measurement of "translational kinetic energy" that represents movement, which can then be assessed for indices of interpersonal coordination, including synchronous movement. For example, motion capture can be used to examine the ratios of total movement in infant-mother dyads, including total infant activity, total maternal activity, total simultaneous movement, and total simultaneous "silence" (periods where infant and mother were both still) for different body regions (head, upper-body, and arms) (Egmose et al., 2017). These scores were calculated as the percentage of time spent in the movement type divided by the total amount of time recorded. They examined associations between these different types of movement synchrony and person-coded interaction quality variables in 4-month-olds infant-mother dyads and identified strong positive associations with movement silence and maternal sensitivity dyadic reciprocity, particularly for arm motions (Egmose et al., 2017).

Other studies using wearable sensors have explored spontaneous movement synchronization with strangers (Cuadros et al., 2019; Cuadros et al., 2020) as opposed to mothers or other familiar adults. Stranger-infant synchrony was examined during storybook reading with 14-month-olds, where a trained experimenter read a storybook aloud to an infant (Cuadros et al., 2019). Both adult and infant were fitted with MoCap markers; the infant wore a sweater and hat that held the markers (two on the back, one on each elbow, and three on the head). A follow up study with 14-month-olds employed the same methodology to determine if there were differences in stranger-infant synchrony that were dependent on whether the synchronization was spontaneous or not (Cuadros et al., 2020). In both of these studies, the sensors on the back were averaged together to form a single time series of position for each participant. Findings from these studies demonstrated that infants in the spontaneous (storybook) setting synchronize their movements to the unfamiliar adult in a mirror-like way – that is, they move the same direction as an adult did (i.e., if the adult moves to their left, the infant moves to their right).

It is also possible to examine the temporal structure of movement synchrony using wearable sensors with an infant population. Two types of ratio scores can be calculated: (1) "coactive onset ratios," defined as "the percentage of (partner A's) movements which occur (a) while (partner B) is moving and (b) within 1.5s after the onset of (partner B) movement" (p. 7, Egmose et al., 2017), and (2) "alternating onset ratios," defined as "the percentage of (partner A's) movements which occur (a) while (partner B) is not moving and (b) within 1.5s after (partner B) movement offset" (p. 7, Egmose et al., 2017). Egmose et al. (2017) differentiate these two scores from a theoretical perspective, suggesting that the alternating onset ratio is representative of turn-taking (i.e., where one person begins moving while the other is still, waiting for their turn to engage) and that the coactive onset ratio is representative of "simultaneous activity" (i.e., where one partner begins moving and that incites the other partner to "join in"). Their findings indicated that for infants at 4 and 13 months, maternal coactive and alternating motion were related to lower levels of dyadic negative states and infant negative affect, but infant coactive and alternating motion ratios were not related to any interaction qualities. These findings suggest that the temporal dynamics of movement synchronization contain meaningful information that helps to discriminate between adaptive and maladaptive interactions, thus suggesting it could be an important feature of infant-mother interaction that should be considered.

Aggregated cross-correlation curves have been used to examine the timing of synchronization during storybook reading (Cuadros et al., 2019). The authors examined cross-correlations between the obtained movement time series for adult and infant using time-lags between −1.5 s and 1.5 s, with 0 s representing simultaneous movement. Negative lag-times were set to represent infant-leading movements (where the infant moved, followed by the adult) and positive lag-times were representative of infant-following movements (where the adult moved, followed by the infant). Two significant correlation peaks were observed in the aggregated cross-correlation curves: one at −0.4 s, with a negative correlation value indicating anatomical coordination (e.g., when the pair is facing each other and the infant moves to their right, the adult also moves to their right – an "opposite" movement – occurring 0.4 s after the infant's movement), and one at 0.9 s, with a positive correlation value indicating mirror-like coordination (i.e., when the pair is facing each other and the adult moves to their left, the infant moves to their right – a "mirrored" movement – occurring 0.9 s after the adult movement). One could also examine the time-lag of movement synchronization using a wider time-lag window (−2 s to 2 s) (Cuadros et al., 2020). Time-lag data for movement synchronization revealed that infants displayed two peaks in the aggregated cross-correlation curves during the spontaneous synchrony condition: one at 0.9 s, and one at 1.5s. However, they displayed none at zero-lag, which would have indicated simultaneous movement synchrony. Conversely, in their forced-synchronization rhythmic bouncing task, they identified significant synchronization at zero-lag, indicating that the participants were moving consistently and simultaneously (Cuadros et al., 2020).

Though they are somewhat outside of the scope of this section, it is important to note that several other human physiological systems that can be captured using wearable sensors and have been known to exhibit synchronization in infant-mother dyads are associated with behavioral measures of infant-mother synchrony (Abney et al., 2021; Feldman, 2006; Feldman et al., 2011) (for recent reviews of infant-mother physiological synchrony, see Davis et al., 2018 and DePasquale, 2020). Most of the popular methods for measuring physiological synchrony (measuring vagal tone and responsiveness, heart rate, skin conductance, finger pulse amplitude, respiration) also employ wearable sensors to collect data from infant and mother simultaneously.

Unfortunately, no matter the modality being measured, wearable sensors can be cumbersome to employ and somewhat limiting. Infants need to tolerate the wearable sensors, and the use of some traditional, more widely available wearable sensors can limit data collection to laboratory-based settings, particularly when specialized equipment is necessary (Bente & Novotny, 2020; Lourenço et al., 2021). Wearable sensor technology can also be expensive, depending on the sensors used and their equipment requirements (Dunbar et al., 2022; Pouw et al., 2020). The body movements of interacting individuals, however, are capable of being captured in a simple video stream. Thus, more recently the field has begun applying computational techniques to video streams to assess movement synchrony.

2.2.2 Computational Assessment of Movement Synchronization

Advances in computer vision methods now allow for marker-less video-based assessment of movement synchronization. Several types of techniques are available that can be applied to a stream of video data for the automatic assessment of movement synchrony, including both traditional computer vision and deep-learning-based 2D pose-estimation algorithms, 3D pose-estimation, and frame-differencing approaches (Leo et al., 2022).

Pose estimation is an attractive alternative to traditional sensor-based motion capture. Motion capture approaches typically require participants to wear markers (either optical or electromagnetic) at specific locations on the body. To implement marker-less pose-estimation, computer vision algorithms are trained to automatically detect key body points across frames in a video stream. A skeleton connecting the body points is superimposed onto the image (see Figure 1), and each key point is tracked in 2D space from frame to frame in the video stream, providing a coordinate location for each point across time. The result is a time series that represents movement for key body parts over the course of an interaction. Popular 2D pose-estimation tools include OpenPose (Cao et al., 2021), DeepLabCut (Mathis et al., 2018), BabyPose (Yurtsever & Eken, 2022) and Alpha-Pose (Fang et al., 2022). To date, very few studies have employed 2D pose estimation to examine synchrony of movement between infant and mother (Jebeli et al., 2024; Klein et al., 2020; Stamate et al., 2023; Stamate et al., 2024), though studies have used them to assess movement synchrony occurring between two adult participants (Fujiwara & Yokomitsu, 2021), between parent and child (Alghowinem et al., 2021; Shin et al., 2022) and within a single infant (intra-limb coordination, Abbasi et al., 2023).

It is also possible to apply pose-estimation to three-dimensional coordinate data. RBG-depth cameras (such as Microsoft Kinect (Hesse et al., 2019; Leclère et al., 2016)) are a low-cost option that can be used to obtain both two- and three-dimensional features of movement, including quantity of movement (2D) and relative orientation of the body to another individual or object (3D) (Leclère et al., 2016). Applying pose estimation to three-dimensional coordinate data can be used to examine movement synchronization occurring in infant-mother dyads in naturalistic play settings. In one study, pose estimation to three-dimensional coordinate data isolated patterns of movement synchronization

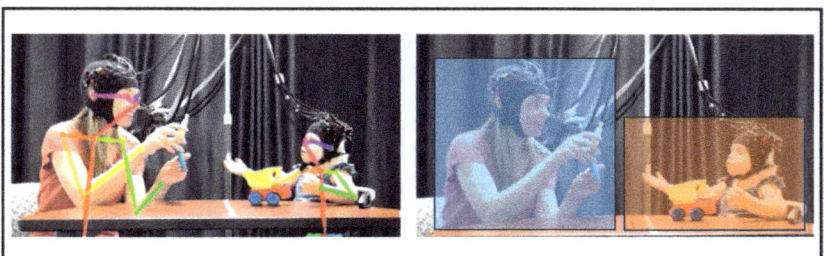

Figure 1 Video-capture of an infant and mother interacting in a free play session.

that were predictive of group membership (neglect-mothers and control-mothers) (Leclère et al., 2016).

Other types of tracking-learning-detection algorithms have been successfully employed with infant-mother dyads. These algorithms are computer vision techniques, trained to detect specific features in a video frame and track them in 2D pixel space across frames, providing a measurement of movement. For example, the CISRO cylinder-based 3D head tracker can track the head movements of mothers and their infants during the Still-Face paradigm (Hammal et al., 2015). This particular tracker detects the head, and within the head determines the position (pitch (vertical direction), yaw (horizontal direction), and roll (lateral direction)) using location of the nose and eyes in relation to the angle of the head. The output is several time series for each participant that represent the angular displacement (the head's movement) and the angular velocity (the speed with which the head was moving) in each plane of movement (pitch, yaw, and roll). Their findings indicated that in the Still-Face paradigm, mother and infant head movements were coupled (as indicated by windowed cross-correlation), with the angular velocity of pitch and yaw more tightly coupled during the play phase compared to the reunion phase. A tracking-learning-detection algorithm (see Kalal et al., 2012 for details) can be used to examine infant head movements (with the direction of the face interpreted as direction of the infant's attention) and mother hand movements (as the mother held and animated an object of interest) (López Pérez et al., 2017). The output of the tracking-learning-detection algorithm is a time series of coordinate positioning for infant and mother, respectively.

Another popular technique used for the assessment of adult-adult movement synchrony is frame-differencing. One frequently employed frame-differencing method is motion energy analysis, which has been used to examine coordination dynamics in therapeutic contexts with adults (Ramseyer & Tschacher, 2011; Ramseyer, 2020). Recently, motion energy analysis has been applied to infant-parent video data for the first time (Hammack et al., 2023). Frame differencing is a technique which quantifies the pixel values of a grayscale video within user-defined regions of interest (ROIs), as shown in Figure 1. It then calculates the change in ROI values from frame to frame. These value changes are considered movements contained within the ROI, which is represented as "motion-energy" (Hammack et al., 2023). Movement synchrony as identified through motion energy analysis has been demonstrated to be associated with movement synchrony measurements obtained using OpenPose in adult therapeutic contexts (Fujiwara & Yokomitsu, 2021). To our knowledge, only our group (Hammack et al., 2023) has successfully employed motion energy analysis with an infant population. In our recent publication, we applied motion energy analysis to examine total-body movement synchrony between infant and mother in a free play setting obtained using a video-conferencing platform (Zoom). We were able to identify positive associations between globally coded measures of behavioral synchrony (using the Coding Interactive Behavior scale; see Section 2.1.2) and dyadic movement synchrony as captured by motion energy analysis, suggesting that when a dyad is moving more synchronously, the mother is exhibiting higher levels of maternal sensitivity, the infant is exhibiting higher levels of involvement, and the dyad is exhibiting higher levels of reciprocal behavior.

2.2.3 Considerations When Employing Automated Methods

Depending on the method employed, one has several considerations when collecting data for later movement assessment. If wearables are being used, it is important to consider the context in which they may be employed. Wearables are generally considered specialized equipment, and therefore require a structured, often lab-based setting, limiting the generalizability of findings outside of these contexts. Additionally, infants need to be able to tolerate the wearable device for the duration of the study or play period being examined, which can be difficult depending on the complexity and design of the wearable device in question (Cornejo et al., 2017).

When collecting data for assessment with computational methods, one must consider the placement of video cameras. One prominent issue with these computational methods is loss of data due to overlapped movement or partial visibility of the participants (Karaca et al., 2024). Algorithms are trained to detect specific features, and often struggle to track consistently if these features become partially occluded. Having several cameras to capture various angles is one way to mitigate this, although in more naturalistic settings it is not always feasible. Depending on the experimental design, the parent may hold the infant in their lap, or the infant and/or parent may even leave the frame entirely (Hammack et al., 2023) resulting in frames that need to be removed from the time series. Another issue that arises is the translation of some of these methods to infant research. Most pose-estimation methods (apart from BabyPose (Yurtsever & Eken, 2022) and few others) are trained on adult physical models; infants have different physical proportions to adults and move in different ways, and thus the algorithms trained on adult models may struggle to track the infant form efficiently when it is in unfamiliar positions or makes sporadic movements (Huang et al., 2021; Karaca et al., 2024).

2.2.4 Analytic Approaches for Movement Time-Series Data

Both wearables and computational methods provide a time series of movement data for each partner (parent and infant) that can be fed into a variety of analytic techniques. Global motion features can be computed by averaging the time series associated with body parts, where movements are categorized into motion features and then collapsed into percentages of time spent in that motion feature. Global motion features are single values that lack a time-domain component; however, they are easily assessed in conjunction with other higher-level constructs. For example, one group of researchers computed activity ratios (i.e., the percentage of time that infant or parent was moving), an overlap ratio (i.e., percentage of time in which both infant and parent were moving at the same time), and a silence ratio (i.e., percentage of time in which no movement occurred). Correlations between these ratios and dyadic interaction qualities, such as maternal sensitivity and infant involvement, as measured by the Coding Interactive Behavior scale (Section 2.1.2 provides more information about the Coding Interactive Behavior scale) were then computed (Egmose et al., 2017).

The extraction of global motion features has limitations. Investigators are not only interested in the global motion features of an interaction, but also the time-dependent features of movement synchronization (e.g., who initiates movement and who follows along, whether different body parts are coordinated across individuals). The research question specifies the way to quantify synchrony, as different methodologies capture different aspects of movement coordination.

There are two types of approaches to analyses of movement time-series data that enable investigators to assess changes in behavior: time domain and frequency domain. Time domain approaches focus on identifying patterns in the data over time. Frequency domain approaches isolate frequency components (i.e., the number of occurrences of a repeating event over a unit of time) and examine how behaviors at different frequencies contribute to the overall signal. Techniques that include both types of approaches can be found in Table 3.

Time-domain approaches. For hypotheses examining whether two individuals exhibit synchronous movement throughout an entire interaction, zero-order correlation (Hammal et al., 2015; Tsai et al., 2011) can serve as a basic metric of synchrony. Zero-order correlation measures the strength and direction of the linear link between two movement time series, resulting in a single correlation coefficient. A positive correlation between two movement time series (e.g., from two people) indicates that as one person moves more, the other also moves more. Alternatively, as one person moves less, the other person also moves less. A negative correlation indicates as one person increases movement the other

Table 3 Comparison of analytic techniques for time-series analysis

Technique	Time Domain	Frequency Domain	Assumes linearity in the time series	Assumes stationarity in the time series	Can test effects of other variables in the model	Provides Information about lead-lag structure	Can provide phase values	Tests direction of influence
Correlational Analyses	X	—	X	X	—	—	—	—
Windowed Crossed-lagged Correlation	X	—	X	X	—	X	—	—
Windowed Crossed-lagged Regression	X	—	X	X	X	X	—	—
Vector Autoregressive Models	X	—	X	X	X	X	—	X
Cross-recurrence Quantification Analysis	X	—	—	—	—	X	—	X
Fourier Analyses	—	X	X	X	—	—	—	—

Table 3 (cont.)

Technique	Time Domain	Frequency Domain	Assumes linearity in the time series	Assumes stationarity in the time series	Can test effects of other variables in the model	Provides Information about lead-lag structure	Can provide phase values	Tests direction of influence
Wavelet Transform Coherence	X	X	—	—	—	X	X	—
Granger Causality Analysis	X	X	—	—	—	—	—	X
Phase-Locking Value and Phase Coherence	X	X	—	—	—	X	—	—
Partial Directed Coherence	X	X	—	—	—	X	—	—
Generalized Partial Directed Coherence	X	X	—	—	—	X	—	X

decreases movement. However, global motion features do not distinguish between simultaneous and delayed movement, nor do they account for fluctuations in synchrony over time.

To mitigate this limitation, researchers often utilize windowed cross-lagged correlation (Cuadros et al., 2019; Cuadros et al., 2020). In cross-lagged correlation, the time series is divided into overlapping windows (e.g., 1–5 sec, 2–6 sec, 3–7 sec). Within each window, the correlation between two signals at different lags is calculated. In other words, one time series is shifted relative to the other and correlations are calculated for the cross-lagged windows. Smaller windows heighten sensitivity to transient fluctuations but may contribute noise, whereas larger windows attenuate variations but may conceal significant coordination changes. The advantage of a cross-lagged correlation approach as compared to a zero-order correlation is that it allows measurement of correlation at various lags over a time series. Limitations of cross-lagged correlations are that they are sensitive to missing data points and do not allow for conclusions to be drawn about the direction of influence of one signal on the other.

A windowed cross-lagged regression (Altmann, 2011; Schoenherr et al., 2019), enhances cross-lagged correlation by using regression models to evaluate how one individual's movement predicts another's over time. Similar to windowed cross-lagged correlation, windowed cross-lagged regression divides time series into segments. Regression analyses are then performed within each window where one time series is used to predict another time series at different lags. The regression analyses can also include other factors, such as baseline measurements of synchrony or maternal traits, highlighting possible causal links. In the context of mother-infant interactions, for example, windowed cross-lagged regression can identify whether a mother's movement predicts her infant's movements (or vice versa) and what factors influence these one-way effects. Similar to windowed cross-lagged correlation, windowed cross-lagged correlation requires careful selection of window lengths and is sensitive to missing data.

Vector autoregressive models offer a more sophisticated method for understanding the reciprocal, time-related effects between infant and parent behaviors (Ngueyep & Serban, 2015). In contrast to windowed cross-correlation, which measures synchronization strength, and windowed cross-lagged regression, which emphasizes one-way directional prediction, vector autoregressive models assess whether past measurements of synchrony can predict future values. In addition, vector autoregressive models incorporate interactions across multiple lags allowing one to assess reciprocal causal relations over time (Ngueyep & Serban, 2015). For instance, vector autoregressive models can reveal whether a mother's touch affects the infant's movement in the following seconds, while also accounting for how the infant's movement influences the mother's future responses. The ability to model dynamic feedback loops enhances our understanding of the change of interactive patterns over time. This is especially relevant for studying co-regulation, where both individuals actively engage in the interaction instead of just reacting to one another. Finally, one might also be interested in identifying the extent to which other measured variables, such as infant states or maternal traits, influence coordinated patterns of behavior.

All of the techniques discussed thus far are linear methods, meaning that they assume that interactions occur at a regular frequency and follow consistent patterns over time. However, natural interactions often involve multiple overlapping rhythms. Different behaviors occur at varying speeds and adapt dynamically to the context in which the interaction occurs. For instance, a mother may nod and smile rhythmically while speaking, while her infant waves their arm in at a different tempo. As the interaction unfolds, these rhythms may change. As a result, traditional linear models may fail to detect subtle shifts in the timing of responses or intermittent coordination patterns.

To overcome these challenges, researchers can employ nonlinear techniques, such as cross-recurrence quantification analysis (Fusaroli et al., 2014). Nonlinear techniques are specifically designed to identify intermittent, event-driven, and nonstationary coordination pattern. Nonstationary refers to a time series in which the statistical properties of the data (e.g., the mean and variance) change over time. If the time series is nonstationary (i.e., does not show a stable pattern over time), past observations may not reliably predict future values. Nonlinear models are particularly useful for analyzing turn-taking in conversations, joint attention episodes, or varying engagement levels in infant-parent interactions. Some nonlinear techniques, such as cross-recurrence quantification analysis, can also accommodate both continuous and categorical data, thereby serving as an effective technique for the analysis of various types of social interaction, including those important for co-regulation of emotion and attachment.

Frequency-domain approaches. One of the challenges of analyzing movement data, particularly data that are collected in naturalistic non-structured contexts, is that different types of movement occur at different frequencies, to which time-domain approaches are agnostic. Frequency domain approaches are designed to capture and assess movements that occur at varying rates. For example, two people dancing together may have different footstep speeds while coordinating arm movements at a completely different rhythm. Time-domain analysis can indicate whether their movements generally align, but it misses the nuance of how these multiple frequencies interact. One well known frequency domain approach is Fourier analysis. Fourier analysis transforms a time-domain signal into its constituent frequencies so that the frequency content of signals can be analyzed (Fujiwara et al., 2020; Schmidt & Fitzpatrick, 2019). One can then test how well the movements of interacting partners align at specific frequencies, or rhythms, during the course of the interaction (Fujiwara et al., 2020; Schmidt & Fitzpatrick, 2019). The frequency-domain perspective is crucial in the study of motor synchrony, as human actions rarely occur at a single frequency, and Fourier analysis can provide a more complete picture of how different motor rhythms synchronize during social interaction (Schmidt & Richardson, 2008).

One limitation of Fourier transform is that it assumes stable frequencies throughout an interaction. In other words, like correlational and regression techniques described earlier, Fourier analysis is constrained by the assumption of stationarity. Hence, Fourier analysis is suitable for structured, repetitive activities, such as rhythmic rocking or bouncing in mother-infant interactions. However, this assumption limits applicability in dynamic, non-repetitive contexts such as spontaneous free play between infant-parent dyads (Issartel et al., 2015; Pukhova et al., 2018).

A technique that does not does not assume stationarity and allows for simultaneous analyses of both time-domain and frequency-domain features is wavelet transform coherence. Wavelet transform coherence breaks down signals into frequency bands, allowing researchers to explore time-based coordinated changes in movement synchrony across a range of rhythmic speeds (Fujiwara & Daibo, 2016; Fujiwara & Yokomitsu, 2021). This is done in several steps. First, wavelet transform decomposes a signal into components at various frequencies, providing a time-frequency representation of the signal; then coherence is calculated. Coherence measures the correlation between two signals at a specific frequency and indicates how well one signal can be predicted from another at that frequency. Wavelet transform coherence combines the wavelet transform with the coherence analysis by calculating the coherence between two signals at different frequencies and times, providing a detailed view of their relation. The result is a time-frequency map that shows when and how the signals are correlated, as illustrated in Figure 2. The wavelet transform coherence plot, often referred to as a heat map, highlights areas of high coherence between the signals at specific times and frequencies. The heat map also provides other information about the relation between the two signals that are not apparent in the time or frequency domain alone. For example, the phase relation between the two signals can take the form of lead-lag synchronization (signal 1 precedes signal 2, or the reverse), in-phase synchronization (the

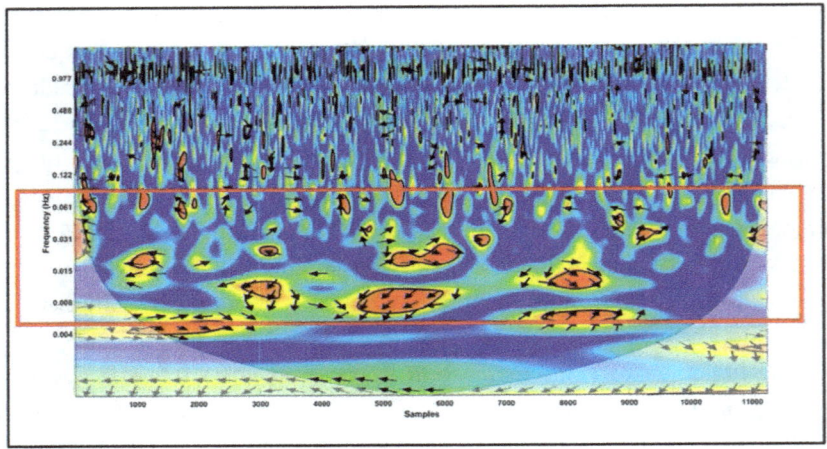

Figure 2 Wavelet transform coherence plot.

peaks and troughs of the two signals align), or anti-phase synchronization (i.e., the peaks of one time series align with the troughs of another.

One concern of which researchers should be aware, independent of the analytic technique used, is how to determine whether coordinated patterns of movement observed in dyads represent true social synchrony and is not incidental (e.g., due to environmental stimuli such as the humming of a fan or common biorhythms). Best practices in the adult literature involve the creation of pseudo dyads which we highly recommend (Fujiwara & Yokomitsu, 2021). Pseudo dyads are created by randomly pairing members of one dyad with those of a different dyad. Then movement synchrony observed in real dyads is compared to that observed in pseudo dyads (i.e., control dyads). More detailed discussion about the value of including pseudo dyads, when analyzing movement time-series data and neural time-series data, can be found in Section 3.1.3 and Section 4.1, respectively.

In summary, there are many different approaches to the analysis of time-series movement data, none of which are inherently right or wrong. The best approach depends on the context in which the data were collected and the research question. For example, if the movement data is repetitive (linear and stationary) and the goal is to establish the extent to which two time series are associated (without drawing conclusions about directionality) a zero-order correlation will suffice. However, many research questions in developmental science involve behavior that is not nonstationary, is observed in conjunction with other nonstationary behavior, and that occurs at a different frequency. One might also be interested in assessing the extent to which other factors (e.g., maternal traits, infant motor abilities, dyadic qualities) influence measures of interpersonal movement synchrony. In these cases, careful consideration of all of these aspects will guide your choices.

3 Neural Measures of Interpersonal Synchrony

The "second-person neuroscience approach" has revolutionized our understanding of human sociability by focusing on real-time reciprocal social interactions (Gvirts, 2020; Hoehl & Markova, 2018; Redcay & Schilbach, 2019). This approach has provided novel insights into neural synchrony, which refers to the coordination of brain activities between individuals during face-to-face engagement (Nguyen et al., 2020; Wass et al., 2020). Synchrony is a bidirectional process, where both the infant and parent mutually influence one another (Schilbach et al., 2013). The groundbreaking technique of hyperscanning, where brain activity is simultaneously recorded in multiple individuals, has opened up new avenues for studying interactions through the measurement of inter-brain correlations (Balconi & Vanutelli, 2018; Bevilacqua et al., 2019; Wass et al., 2020). The application of hyperscanning sheds light on the neural processes that underlie social cognition and communication as well as the dynamics of social interactions (Gvirts & Perlmutter, 2020; Hamilton, 2021).

In the field of naturalistic, applied neuroscience, hyperscanning studies offer a variety of techniques (e.g., fNIRS, EEG, fMRI, MEG), each with unique advantages. However, functional near-infrared spectroscopy (fNIRS) stands out as a particularly noteworthy technique for use with infant populations. Recent advancements in fNIRS technology have led to the development of wearable, wireless high-density systems, expanding the possibilities for studying brain activity in various scenarios including, for example, naturalistic infant-mother interactions. Technological advancements have also increased the portability of fNIRS devices, allowing for investigations of human face-to-face interactions in naturalistic environments like families' homes or specialized clinical settings, thereby enhancing the authenticity and relevance of the findings. Additionally, fNIRS exhibits reduced susceptibility to motion artifacts compared to electroencephalography (EEG), allowing participants to engage in natural movements during social interactions with less compromise to data quality, an important consideration when working with infants who cannot be instructed to stay still. Although EEG has greater temporal resolution than fNIRS, the latter has greater spatial localization. Finally, fNIRS allows for assessment of regional hemodynamic activity from the cortical surface, providing researchers with valuable insights into key brain regions and neural systems relevant to social neuroscience.

When designing studies, researchers must identify cortical regions of interest. Our understanding of the cortical areas involved in interpersonal dyadic synchrony in the developing brain is still evolving, but we can draw insights from single-brain studies that investigated socio-cognitive processes relevant to interpersonal synchrony. For example, when infants observe an adult signaling communicative intent through joint attention, gaze direction, or pointing, it activates regions in the prefrontal cortex (PFC) (Grossman & Johnson, 2010; Grossman et al., 2010). In addition, the processing of others' belief states activates the temporoparietal junction (TPJ), and this pattern of activation in infancy predicts reasoning about other's thoughts and beliefs later in childhood (Hyde et al., 2018; Liu et al., 2025). Comprehensive reviews of single-brain studies provide more detailed information on the neural underpinnings of socio-cognitive processes relevant to interpersonal synchrony (e.g., Ilyka et al., 2021; McDonald & Perdue, 2018).

We can also gain insight into potential regions of interest from research conducted with adults. Models proposed in the adult literature suggest that social alignment is mediated by a network of cortical areas that work together to achieve and regulate interpersonal synchrony (Gvirts & Perlmutter, 2020; Shamay-Tsoory et al., 2019). According to Gvirts' and Perlmutter's version of this model, the neural basis of social alignment includes several key systems, including the mutual social attention, gap monitoring, and gap monitoring systems (Gvirts & Perlmutter, 2020). The mutual social attention system is associated with the temporoparietal junction (TPJ) and promotes mutual attention between interacting partners. The gap monitoring system is associated with the dorsomedial prefrontal cortex (dmPFC) and anterior cingulate cortex (ACC). This system detects misalignment between one's own movements, thoughts, and emotions, and those of others. The observation execution system is located in the inferior frontal gyrus (IFG) and inferior parietal lobe (IPL) and facilitates the alignment of one's own movements, thoughts, and emotions with others.

Supporting the Gvirts and Perlmutter (2020) model, studies with adults have shown that brain coupling occurs in the inferior frontal gyrus and dorsomedial prefrontal cortex during dyadic interactions (Marton-Alper et al., 2023) and that activation in prefrontal areas is associated with behavioral synchrony during these interactions (Jiang et al., 2012). Additionally, activation in the dorsomedial prefrontal cortex is particularly strong during tasks that require greater attention to aligning one's behavior with another's (Marton-Alper et al., 2023).

Findings from fNIRS hyperscanning studies with infants and children, although limited, are consistent with Gvirts and Perlmutter's (2020) conceptual model. For example, in infants aged 4–6 months, synchrony has been observed in the inferior frontal gyrus and the medial prefrontal cortex during free play tasks (Nguyen, Zimmer et al., 2023). Older infants, from 9 to 24 months, exhibit activation in the prefrontal cortex and temporoparietal areas, including the temporoparietal junction, during similar tasks (Morgan et al., 2023; Piazza et al., 2020). This pattern continues in children aged 4–6 years, with studies reporting activation in the dorsolateral prefrontal cortex and temporoparietal junction (Li et al., 2024; Nguyen, Hoehl et al., 2021).

The brain regions targeted depends on the socio-cognitive processes thought to be engaged during interpersonal synchronization. Selecting brain regions tied to behavioral outcomes enhances the interpretability of fNIRS data. As a case in point, infant researchers have found that interbrain synchrony in the prefrontal cortex and temporoparietal junction is closely associated with the presence of social behaviors that enhance communication. For example, instances of direct gaze and smiling, which attract a partner's attention and indicate the intent to share information, are linked to interbrain synchrony in the prefrontal cortex (Nguyen, Zimmer et al., 2023; Piazza et al., 2020). Additionally, instances of joint attention and turn-taking are connected to interbrain synchrony in the temporoparietal junction (Morgan et al., 2023).

3.1 Hyperscanning Using fNIRS

Given the unique advantages of using fNIRS in the developmental sciences, there are a growing number of studies that have employed hyperscanning using fNIRS in the infant population. fNIRS data collection with infants can be challenging; researchers may need to exclude dyads from their dataset because of infant fatigue, fussiness, inability to tolerate the headgear, procedural problems (e.g., poor headgear placement or interruptions during the experimental session), or failure to complete the experimental task. In addition, data quality may be compromised by excessive motion artifacts and/or low signal to noise ratio. In this section, we will give suggestions for mitigating the challenges that accompany conducting fNIRS hyperscanning experiments with infants and young children.

Recall that most infant research investigating interpersonal synchrony has been conducted with infant-mother dyads, largely because mothers are more accessible research participants than fathers or other caregivers. Some but not all studies including both mothers and fathers have reported differences in the way that mothers and fathers coordinate with their infants (e.g., Feldman, 2007;

Liu, Zhu et al., 2024; Nguyen, Schleihauf et al., 2021). In addition, the extent to which differences between infant-mother and infant-father dyads are observed may vary by context and the way in which synchrony is measured. Hence, it is important to consider whether parent gender-related differences are expected and whether you have access to a sufficient number of infant-father and infant-mother dyads to conduct a balanced design. Although recruiting a sufficient number of infant-father dyads to have a balanced design is challenging, it is critical to the generalizability of the findings.

3.1.1 Study Design, Experimental Setup, Montage Construction

Hyperscanning studies are typically performed during naturalistic interactions of about 5–10 minutes and include a baseline period, which is generally tolerable for infants and young children. However, if multiple interaction types (i.e., multiple trial types) are to be employed in a testing session, the length of each trial will need to be adjusted to maintain the infant's engagement and minimize fussiness. We recommend that each session not exceed over 20 minutes of active infant engagement in the experimental tasks (and perhaps no more than 45 minutes spent in the fNIRS cap, including time for experimenter instruction). For newborns and very young infants who do not yet have the ability to sit up unsupported, an infant car seat or other arrangement that provides full postural support is required. For older infants and toddlers that can sit up on their own, a highchair may suffice. We advise video-recording the session to ensure quality of fNIRS data collection; researchers can use the video data to review and flag moments when neural data collection has been compromised (such as moments of excessive movement, participant touching the headgear, fussiness from the infant). Video-recordings are also beneficial if coding behavioral data is important to the analysis and interpretation of fNIRS data (see Section 4.2.1). Figure 3 shows an arrangement that we use in our lab for infant-parent testing.

Prior to collecting hyperscanning data, the researcher should determine the appropriate position and arrangement of the optodes by designing the headgear montage. This step is critical to ensuring that one obtains an optimal signal from the cortical areas of interest (see Yücel et al., 2021). One can choose to use preset configurations made available by NIRStar (NIRStar v.205 software) or similar programs, or one can choose to create a customized configuration. Of similar importance, it is necessary to select a headgear design that is tolerable for an infant participant by considering both the number of fibers and the weight of the fibers that will be included in the montage. We advise organizing the fibers in such a way that facilitates quick headgear placement on the infant (who are less patient than adult participants) and facilitates protection of the fibers

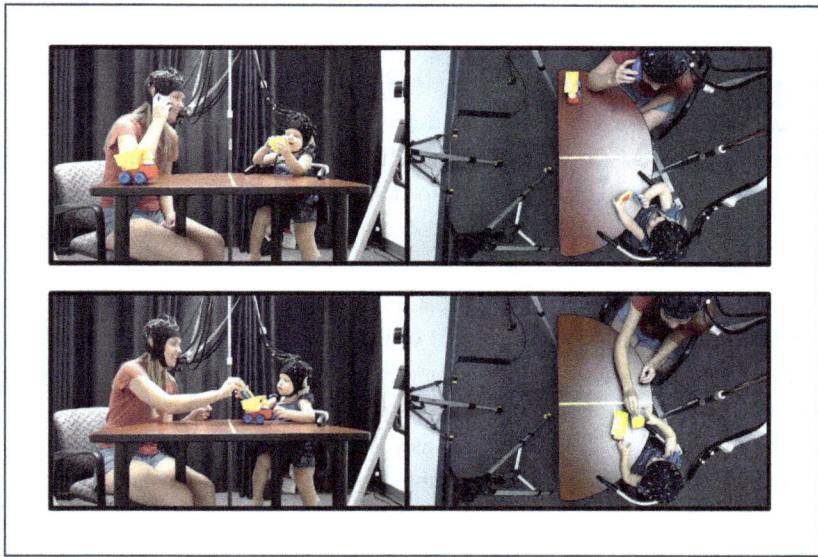

Figure 3 Experimental set-up for an infant-parent dyadic synchrony test session.

throughout the experimental session from handsy infants. For example, fibers can be grouped into bundles and carefully placed/affixed behind each member of the dyad.

During data collection, it is essential that the headgear placement is standardized across all the participants. To this end, researchers can locate and mark external anatomical landmarks on the infant and parent heads, such as the nasion, inion, vertex, and the bilateral preauricular points. By using the 10–20 (or similar) system for identifying brain regions, researchers can ensure that the cap localizations correspond to the anatomical landmarks (Filippetti et al., 2023; Piazza et al., 2019; Quiñones-Camacho et al., 2019; Reindl et al., 2019). Some researchers also choose to complete an optode registration, which is done when the researcher registers the participant's MRI scans with software that can determine the anatomical location of brain areas for each participant (Hoyniak et al., 2021; Quinones-Camacho et al., 2019; Theyer et al., 2024). Alternatively, when MRI scans are not available, researchers can register functional brain data to software that can simulate probable MNI coordinate values to determine anatomical locations of brain areas (see Minagawa et al., 2023; Tsuzuki et al., 2007).

Once the cap is placed according to the correct anatomical landmarks, one should check each optode for optimal contact with the scalp and adjust as needed (Azhari et al., 2019, 2021; Hoyniak et al., 2021; Quiñones-Camacho et al., 2019). Some researchers perform optode registration (localization of the cap montage on the participants' skull) through the use of a 3D digitizer (i.e., Polhemus Digitising System, http://polhemus.com/scanning-digitizing/digitizing-products/http://polhemus.com/scanning-digitizing/digitizing-products/).

Optode registration is beneficial as it promotes consistent recording from the same brain areas across the participants. However, optode registration in three-dimensional space is often difficult to do with infants because it requires the infant to be still and can be time-consuming (Lloyd-Fox et al., 2014). An alternative option for optode registration could be the recently published STORM-Net (Erel et al., preprint), a system which allows the user to take a quick video (~5 seconds in length) of the participant wearing the headgear. STORM-Net applies computer vision technology and is able to localize the placement of the optodes on the participant in relation to the locations expected, similar to that of a 3D digitizer such as a Polhemus.

We recommend placing and adjusting headgear on the adult participant prior to the infant participant to reduce the amount of time the infant must wear the cap. Distracting the infant with toys, movies, or other activities infants find engaging facilitates successful cap placement and requires teamwork (e.g., one research assistant distracts the infant while another quickly places the headgear cap on the infant infant's head). One can also enlist the parent to help engage the infant and distract them during cap placement. Once the cap is placed according to the correct anatomical landmarks, one should check each optode for optimal contact with the scalp and adjust as needed (Azhari et al., 2019, 2021; Hoyniak et al., 2021; Quinones-Camacho et al., 2019). Next, signal quality should be reviewed with a calibration test (Azhari et al., 2021; Azhari, Bizzego, & Esposito, 2022), which is typically performed on the data collection software provided by the maker of the fNIRS hardware, and headgear adjustments should be conducted to improve signal quality if needed (Hoyniak et al., 2021; Reindl et al., 2019). Note that secure placement of the headgear on the infant and parent can help decrease the opportunity for motion artifacts (e.g., due to torque or tipping of the optodes against the scalp or swinging fibers) and poor signal to noise ratio (e.g., due to poor optode-scalp contact or ambient light).

3.1.2 Data Collection and Pre-processing

Researchers should take care to follow best practices in fNIRS data collection and preprocessing to ensure the quality and reliability of their findings. Most researchers conducting hyperscanning in the developmental sciences use a continuous wave device to collect neural data and employ wavelengths between 690 nm and 850 nm (e.g., Azhari, Bizzego, Balagtas et al., 2022; Bizzego et al., 2022; Filippetti et al., 2023; Nguyen, Kungl et al., 2023). Oxygenated hemoglobin

(HBO) and de-oxygenated hemoglobin (HBR) have similar absorption coefficients at about 800 nm, so a wavelength below 780 nm and above 830 nm is considered optimal pairing to assess HBR and HBO, respectively (Scholkmann et al., 2014). Dependent upon the system used for fNIRS data collection, data are typically sampled at a rate of 7.81 Hz (Azhari, Bizzego, & Esposito, 2022; Barreto et al., 2021; Bizzego et al., 2022; Nguyen, Kungl et al., 2023; Oku et al., 2022), or 10 Hz (Emberson et al., 2017; Filippetti et al., 2023), providing sufficient temporal resolution to capture the hemodynamic response in infants and adults. Recording can be conducted using a single fNIRS device in hyperscanning mode or by using multiple fNIRS machines in a tandem hyperscanning mode (Nguyen, Kungl et al., 2023). Markers that indicate the start and end of each trial should be recorded in the neural data. Such markers should be synchronized across all modalities of data collection, for example, in the case of audio/visual or physiological data collection. This may be done by sending triggers that mark onsets of specific behaviors, originating at the computer collecting the neural data to any additional computers being used to collect other modalities of data via a parallel port, serial port, or Ethernet cable (the setup of such time-locked trigger systems are dependent on the type of data being collected). Researchers can also use an audio cue (such as saying the words "begin" and "the end") or a visual cue (such as flashing a light toward the camera) to indicate when onsets and offset markers are being entered into the neural recording and to standardize the NIRS data with data of another modality, such as video data.

After data collection is complete, researchers should then employ a comprehensive preprocessing pipeline to ensure the quality and reliability of their functional near-infrared spectroscopy (fNIRS) data. This pipeline typically involves several critical steps such as: (1) conversion from intensity to optical density data, (2) visual inspection of the signals and/or signal quality tests for removal of poor channels, (3) motion artifact correction, (4) bandpass filtering, (5) applying a partial pathlength factor, and (6) conversion from optical density data to oxyhemoglobin and deoxyhemoglobin. Current methodological papers offer more detailed information about best practices for pre-processing infant fNIRS data (e.g., Gemignani & Gervain, 2021) and for pre-processing infant/child-parent fNIRS hyperscanning data (e.g., Nguyen, Hoehl et al., 2021). A thorough preprocessing pipeline ensures that the fNIRS data is of high quality and suitable for subsequent analyses, enhancing the validity of the study's findings.

3.1.3 Measures of Interbrain Coupling

Brain signals obtained from neuroimaging techniques such as fNIRS and EEG are time-series data. Thus, measures of interbrain coupling require techniques that support the coupling of two time series. Some of the techniques described in Section 2.2.4 have been applied to brain signals. However, there are considerations related to the complexity of neural signals that render some of the techniques described in Section 2.2.4 less-than-appropriate. For example, correlational techniques can be influenced by variations in the shape of the hemodynamic response function as measured by fNIRS. This is problematic because the shape of hemodynamic response functions can differ across individuals of the same age, across different age groups, and across different brain regions (West et al., 2019). EEG signals are also nonstationary, rendering correlational techniques unsuitable. In this section we cover techniques that are considered more appropriate for analysis of neural data. Although the focus of this Element is fNIRS data, we briefly review approaches to the analysis of EEG data as examples of analytic approaches to time-series data.

Interbrain coupling of fNIRS data. In the field of fNIRS hyperscanning wavelet transform coherence has become the standard analytical approach for assessing interbrain synchrony (Czeszumski et al., 2020; Nguyen, Hoehl et al., 2021). Wavelet transform coherence was first introduced in the fNIRS literature in a cooperative and competitive button-press task involving pairs of adult participants (Cui et al., 2012). The researchers quantified brain-to-brain coupling by calculating wavelet transform coherence. Increased coherence in the right superior frontal cortices during a cooperative task, but not during a competitive task, was associated with better cooperation performance (Cui et al., 2012). Wavelet transform coherence has now been applied in adult (Czeszumski et al., 2022) and infant (Nguyen, Abney et al., 2021) populations.

One advantage of wavelet transform coherence is that it computes coherence and phase lag between two time series. Hence, it has been widely applied in domains in which understanding lead-lag structure is important, such as action monitoring, cooperative and competitive behavior, imitation, mother-infant problem-solving, and teaching-learning behavior (Liu et al., 2019; Lu et al., 2021; Pan et al., 2020; Sun et al., 2020; Zhu et al., 2022). Another advantage of wavelet transform coherence is that does not assume stationarity and integrates time- and frequency-domain data (see Section 2.2.4), allowing greater flexibility in the types of situations in which it can be applied. Wavelet transform coherence is also less affected by interregional differences in the hemodynamic response function than other techniques, such as window cross-lagged correlations or vector autoregressive models.

Less well known is that wavelet transform coherence can also provide information about the phase relation between two signals. For example, two neural signals can be in-phase (show activation at the same time) or anti-phase (one brain shows increased activity while the other shows decreased activity).

Historically, research using wavelet transform coherence to evaluate interbrain synchrony failed to distinguish between in-phase and anti-phase interactions and instead used absolute values only. As a result, elevated coherence values may have resulted from both forms of neural synchronization (in-phase and anti-phase), but researchers lacked the means to differentiate between them. Consequently, studies may have inadvertently grouped together fundamentally distinct synchronization patterns, rendering results regarding brain-to-brain connectivity difficult to interpret.

Recently, we introduced a toolbox that enhances phase analysis in wavelet transform coherence, enabling more precise classification of inter-brain synchrony (Gvirts et al., 2023). Our toolbox differentiates between four different synchronization patterns. Specifically, it identifies in-phase synchronization (simultaneous neural activation), lagged synchronization (signal 1 leads signal 2, or the reverse), and anti-phase synchronization (one brain increasing activity while the other decreases). Information about how to access and use the toolbox can be found in Gvirts et al. (2023). Phase distinctions are critical considering the types of interactions in which infants and adults typically engage during naturalistic social interactions. For example, an infant and mother who take turns patting the table (and remain still when it is not their turn) are likely to show anti-phase patterns, whereas an infant and mother who mirror each other are likely to show in-phase neural patterns. The distinction between these two types of interaction patterns would not be detectable using wavelet transform coherence without a method for extracting phase information, which can be accomplished using our toolbox.

Wavelet transform coherence does not provide information about the causal relation between two signals, however. A technique that can be used to investigate causality, which is often referred to as direction of influence, is Granger causality analysis (Granger, 1969). Granger causality analysis quantifies how well one time series can predict another, providing insight into the information flow between brain signals from two interacting brains during social interactions. When wavelet transform coherence is used together with Granger causality analysis, these combined methods provide a more comprehensive understanding of the complex nature of social interactions and interpersonal brain coupling.

Granger causality analysis is more commonly used in adult studies, where it has identified directional coupling in romantic partners (Zhang et al., 2023) and dyads engaged in cooperative (Pan et al., 2017; Zhao et al., 2022) and creative problem-solving tasks (Duan et al., 2022). The application of Granger causality analysis in adult hyperscanning fNIRS studies has yielded insights into the directionality and patterns of information exchange between individuals engaged in social interactions. It represents a promising, yet underexplored, approach for assessing signal coupling in infant-mother dyads assessed with fNIRS hyperscanning.

Researchers should be aware that the approaches we described in Section 2.2.4 and in this section provide information about coordinated changes in two signals over time. However, researchers often calculate a global measure of synchrony by collapsing the obtained values across task-related time blocks and frequency bands into a single representation of inter-brain coherence, limiting their ability to distinguish between different forms of inter-brain synchrony. Recently, there has been increased focus on measures that maintain information about changes in the coordination of two signals over time, particularly in the adult fNIRS literature (Duan et al., 2022; Zhao et al., 2022;). We are eager to see methods that preserve the temporal dynamics of cortical responses applied in developmental sciences (Gvirts et al., 2023; Marriott Haresign et al., 2023).

Interbrain coupling of EEG data. EEG techniques measure changes in electrical activity with millisecond precision. This contrasts with fNIRS which measure changes in hemodynamic responses, which occur at a much slower rate of 2–5 seconds. Many of the methods discussed earlier can also be used with EEG data. However, there are methods designed for fast oscillatory signals and hence well suited for analyzing EEG data.

Frequently used approaches to the analysis of EEG hyperscanning data include phase-locking value and phase coherence. Briefly, phase-locking value measures the degree to which the phase difference between signals remains constant over time. If the two signals are synchronized, the phase differences between them should remain relatively constant. To compute phase-locking value, EEG signals are filtered to isolate the frequency band of interest. Phase-locking value is then calculated as the average of the phase differences across multiple epochs, or time windows. Phase-locking values range from 0 (no phase synchrony) to 1 (perfect phase synchrony). In comparison, phase coherence measures the consistency over time of the phase difference between two signals within a specific frequency band. Both phase-locking value and phase coherence can provide information about lead-lag structure. There are several reviews comparing these approaches, and provide more detailed information (e.g., Czeszumski et al., 2020; Marriott Haresign et al., 2022).

One limitation of phase-locking value and phase coherence is that they do not assess direction of influence between the two signals. Approaches that measure both magnitude and causal relations include partial directed coherence and generalized partial directed coherence. For example, using generalized partial directed coherence, one infant-parent hyperscanning studying identified a bidirectional influence of parent's brain activity on their infant's brain activity during live interactions, particularly during instances of direct gaze between them (Leong et al., 2017). The main difference between partial directed coherence and generalized partial directed coherence is how coherence is calculated. Generalized partial directed coherence incorporates a normalization process that considers the strength of coherence across multiple pairs of signals, and generalized partial directed coherence does not incorporate a normalization process. This normalization process facilitates comparison of connection strengths from different pairs of signals. For example, when measuring synchrony at multiple brain regions during infant-parent interactions, researchers can normalize signals obtained from one location by accounting for the magnitude of synchrony obtained in signals obtained at a different location (Leong et al., 2017). A review of these and other approaches used to measure the temporal dynamics of interpersonal synchrony in infant-parent EEG hyperscanning data can be found in Marriott Haresign et al. (2024).

The importance of pseudo dyads. Once you have a measure of interbrain coupling, you will want to test whether observed synchrony is of a meaningful amplitude and/or whether the amplitude varies significantly across experimental conditions. Comparison of real dyads to pseudo dyads is considered best practice to ensure that observed neural synchrony is due to genuine social interaction rather than other factors. For example, low-level stimulus (e.g., lights flickering or sounds generated by a fan) and coincidental synchrony (e.g., partners who have similar bio-rhythms) can result in spontaneous associations of brain activity between dyadic partners. Typically, pseudo dyads are created by randomly pairing members of true dyads with members of other true dyads (Nguyen, Hoehl et al., 2021; Reindl et al., 2019). For example, infant from dyad 1 can be paired with mother from dyad 2. Some researchers have taken a "shuffled dyad" approach, where moms and infants are randomly shuffled one time so that you have the same number of pseudo and real dyads. We recommend a permutation approach that includes as many permutations as possible. Including all possible permutations, for example, will minimize biases that could arise from specific pairings, allow for a more accurate baseline comparison, and increase statistical power.

4 Interpersonal Synchrony: Coupling of Behavior and Brain

Behavioral studies have significantly enhanced our understanding of early emerging infant-parent synchrony, and the important role synchronized, integrated dyadic interactions play in social, cognitive, and linguistic developmental outcomes (see Section 2 for a detailed discussion of these methods). The introduction of hyperscanning provides another method to study this universal phenomenon that fosters positive developmental outcomes (see Section 3 for more on techniques appropriate for hyperscanning data). However, interpreting hyperscanning data poses challenges, as it is difficult to make sense of coordinated changes in two brain signals without behavioral context. Methods to assess the relationship between behavioral and neural measures of interpersonal synchrony are still underdeveloped. This section will examine approaches that have been used to explore brain-behavior relations during dyadic interactions, shedding light on the bidirectional influences on early patterns of interpersonal synchrony. Illustrative examples of these approaches will be provided.

4.1 Neural Synchrony as a Function of Task Demands

This approach investigates the extent to which measures of neural synchrony vary as a function of the task, or context, in which it is observed. The rationale is that different types of interpersonal interactions may have different processing demands, which will be reflected in the cortical responses observed (e.g., degree of brain synchrony observed and/or the cortical areas in which synchrony is instantiated). Inclusion of behavioral or performance measures, which provide a more detailed assessment of the cognitive and social processes engaged, during the task is optimal. This allows for a stronger interpretation of the relation between task demands and interbrain synchrony.

One example of this approach is to compare neural synchrony in infant/child-parent dyads during an interactive task relative to a task in which members of the dyad are in close proximity but do not interact. To illustrate, researchers have compared child-adult neural synchrony obtained during a cooperative, problem-solving task relative to a task in which the dyads worked independently and out of view of each other (Li et al., 2024; Liu, Han et al., 2024; Nguyen et al., 2020; Nguyen, Schleihauf, Kungl et al., 2021). Greater neural synchrony was observed in frontal and temporoparietal areas during the cooperative as compared to independent task, a finding that also has been observed with adolescent-parent and adult-adult dyads (Lu et al., 2019; Miller et al., 2019). Researchers using this approach typically assess the relation between global measures of neural synchrony (i.e., synchrony averaged over a time series, for each task independently) and other factors of interest, including infant and parent traits (e.g., infant temperament, parental sensitivity), infant and parent states (e.g., stress), and global behavioral measures that capture the quality of the infant-parent interactions (e.g., behavioral reciprocity). Finally, behaviors thought to facilitate socially coordinated interactions, such as touching or eye gaze, can be micro-coded and the frequency with which they occur tabulated (Nguyen, Abney, & Salamander et al., 2021; Papoutselou et al., 2024). One can then test the association between the frequency of target behaviors, putative measures of the socio-cognitive processes engaged as a function of task demands, and the magnitude of the neural synchrony observed.

Another example of the "neural synchrony as a function of task demands" approach is to compare neural synchrony obtained in infant/child-parent dyads in two interactive tasks that are expected to elicit different patterns of interpersonal synchrony (Leong et al., 2017; Minagawa et al., 2023; Reindl et al., 2018; for older children-parent dyads see Reindl et al., 2022). To build on the illustration from earlier, one could compare neural synchrony obtained during a task in which dyads work cooperatively as compared to a task in which dyads work competitively (Reindl et al., 2018). One could also assess the relation between performance measures (e.g., task completion, reaction times) and neural synchrony. With careful experimental design, one could identify the extent to which two different tasks, that engage different socio-cognitive processes, elicit different patterns of interbrain synchrony. Although experimental designs expected to elicit dissociations are not commonly implemented in the developmental literature, at least to date, predictions could be made. For example, fMRI single-brain studies with adults have identified that when playing computer games involving a cooperative versus competitive mindset, a distinct but overlapping pattern of neural activation involving frontal and parietal areas is observed (Decety et al., 2004). On the basis of these findings, one might expect hyperscanning studies to reveal distinct patterns of interbrain synchrony in cooperative as compared to competitive tasks.

We offer a few methodological suggestions for investigators who take this approach. First, when multiple tasks are used, the tasks should differ only on the variable of interest. If the tasks vary on other dimensions (e.g., the types of materials to which the dyads are exposed, the behavioral modality required, or whether members of the dyad sit facing each other or side-by-side), it is difficult to draw strong conclusions about what led to the differences in interpersonal synchrony that were observed. Second, it is critical to ensure that interpersonal synchrony observed was induced by one or more of the experimental manipulations and cannot be attributed to shared low-level stimulus or coincidental synchrony related to individual bio-rhythms, both of which can result in spontaneous associations of brain activity between the dyad members. (This was discussed in Section 3.1.3 but is worth repeating.) To control for this possibility, random permutation analyses or "shuffled pair" analyses are often implemented (Nguyen, Hoehl et al., 2021; Reindl et al., 2019; Reindl et al., 2022). Random permutations and shuffled pairs create pseudo dyads by randomly pairing participants while holding condition constant, representing a baseline for comparison of true dyads to pseudo dyads in each condition, This is important because even when experimental, control, and/or baseline (rest) conditions are included, spurious correlations in the signal can be obtained (Nazneen et al., 2022). For example, some researchers have reported the degree to which interbrain synchrony is observed in an experimental versus a control condition may differ significantly, while at the same time a comparison of interbrain synchrony observed in true versus pseudo dyads within an experimental condition can fail to reach significance (Nguyen, Hoehl et al., 2021).

Third, it is important to carefully select the analytic technique. As outlined in Section 3.1.3, the prevailing approach for assessing interbrain synchrony involves using wavelet transform coherence to assess the strength of signal coupling, typically averaging coherence values across the duration of the interaction. However, using wavelet transform coherence without considering the accompanying phase angle values prevents more nuanced aspects of synchrony from being explored. That is, although one may be able to detect the presence and strength of brain signal coupling between members of a dyad, without phase angles one cannot draw conclusions about the nature of the coupling (e.g., lead-lag structure or whether the neural signals were in-phase or anti-phase). In addition, wavelet transform coherence alone will not provide information about direction of influence. Another technique, such as Granger causality analysis, would need to be included to draw conclusions about the extent to which one signal predicts another other. As the field progresses, we expect to see more nuanced predictions about the effect of task demands on patterns of neural synchrony, requiring more sophisticated analytic techniques for hypothesis testing.

4.2 Behavior-locked and Epoch-locked Approaches to the Coupling of Brain and Behavior

To conduct more fine-grained analyses of the coupling of behavior and brain during dyadic interactions requires implementation of tools that can assess the relation between these two within the temporal dimension. One approach is to assess changes in neural synchrony as a function of changes in behavior that one or both members of the dyad display during a test session (behavior-locked approach). Another approach is to assess changes in behavioral and neural synchrony at experimenter-determined intervals over the course of the interaction (epoch-locked approach).

4.2.1 Behavior-locked Approaches to Brain-Behavior Coupling

A behavior-locked approach investigates changes in interbrain synchrony in relation to the onset of specific behaviors that occur naturally within a dyadic interaction or in response to externally presented stimuli or events (Marriott

Haresign et al., 2024 refer to this as an event-locked approach). This approach typically involves micro-coding specific behaviors of interest (e.g., mutual gaze, joint attention) and then assessing patterns of neural activation during the expression of these behaviors (Liu, Han et al., 2024; Marriott Haresign et al., 2023; Piazza et al., 2020; Wass et al., 2020). To illustrate one application of this approach, Piazza and colleagues (Piazza et al., 2020) assessed neural synchrony in 9- to 15-month-old infants and an adult partner during a together condition (i.e., infant sat in their mother's lap and engaged in free play with an adult experimenter) and an apart condition (i.e., experimenter turned away to engage with another adult and infant sat quietly in mother's lap). During the together condition, incidents of mutual gaze (i.e., joint eye contact), joint attention (i.e., both members of the dyad attended to an external object), and infant smiling were coded. FNIRS time-series data were matched to the time series during which coded behaviors were observed, while accounting for the hemodynamic lag of 4–5s.

Significant coupling of infant-parent neural responses (i.e., interbrain synchrony as measured by correlational analyses) was obtained in channels positioned over PFC and preceded moments of mutual gaze and infant smiling. In addition, an increase in adult PFC activation only preceded incidents of infant-initiated joint attention to objects. Importantly, control analyses in which the neural time series of one member of a dyad was randomly assigned to the behavioral times of a member of a different dyad showed no significant brain-behavior relationships. Finally, regression analyses performed on the behavior-locked infant-adult interbrain synchrony scores revealed that mutual gaze and infant smiling contributed more to the variance in neural coupling than joint attention to objects. That is, mutual gaze and infant smiling were better predictors of interbrain synchrony than joint attention.

Interestingly, another research group also using a behavior-locked approach but with EEG data (Marriott Haresign et al., 2023), reported that with 12-month-old infants and their mothers, gaze onset was not linked to changes in interbrain synchrony. However, the onset of gaze to a social partner was linked to changes within the sender's but not the receiver's brain activity, suggesting that (at least in this study with this age group) intra-brain activity was more closely related to changes in gaze than interbrain activity. There are a number of possible explanations for the apparent discrepancy in results reported by these two studies (e.g., older and more experienced infant inter-actors are better at interpreting social cues or, alternatively, the temporal locking of ostensive signals and interbrain synchrony differs for dyads including older as compared to younger infants). Regardless of the outcome of future work, this is an excellent illustration of the contribution that behavior-locked approaches can make to our conceptual models of interpersonal synchrony, early communicative understanding, and behavior.

4.2.2 Epoch-locked Approaches to Brain-Behavior Coupling

An epoch-locked approach investigates changes in interbrain synchrony across the temporal dimension. In this approach, the duration of a task is divided into time intervals, or epochs, of equal duration. Changes in interbrain synchrony as the epochs progress are then assessed. Typically, behaviors of interest are also micro-coded and the relation between the frequency with which these behaviors are observed and neural synchrony, during each epoch, is calculated (Azhari, Bizzego, & Esposito, 2022; Bizzego et al., 2022; Nguyen, Schleihauf, Kayhan et al., 2021). This approach allows investigators to assess the extent to which neural and behavioral manifestations of interpersonal synchrony change over the course of an interaction. To illustrate this approach, one group of investigators (Nguyen, Zimmer et al., 2023) micro-coded instances of turn-taking, a universal temporal structure important to effective dyadic communication, during each 1-minute epoch of a 5-minute free play session in infants aged 4- to 6-month-old and their mothers. More frequent turn-taking was associated with greater interbrain synchrony in bilateral medial prefrontal cortex. However, the strength of this relation decreased over the course of the interaction (i.e., was greater in early as compared to later epochs).

Curiously, a different pattern of results was obtained in 5-year-olds using a similar procedure (Nguyen, Schleihauf, Kayhan et al., 2021). With the 5-year-olds, turn-taking was positively correlated with neural synchrony in prefrontal cortex, and this increased in later (as compared to earlier) epochs of a 4-minute free play session. These findings hint, again, at possible changes in brain-behavior coupling during social interactions over the first 5 years of life. Turn-taking requires attention to a social partner and coordination of one's own behavior with the partner. It is possible that the rhythmic coordination across behavior and brain signals required for turn-taking emerges gradually during the first few years of life, with older children as compared to younger infants showing more sustained performance over the course of an interaction. Regardless of whether this hypothesis is eventually supported, this illustrates how an epoch-locked approach can reveal not only changes over the course of an interaction, but developmental changes over time and experience.

One practical consideration when implementing a behavior-locked or epoch-locked approach is that coding infant and parent behaviors during the course of an interaction is a laborious task, requiring multiple coders who have been trained to reliability and many hours of coding work. One solution to this challenge is to employ automated coding techniques, as we will report in the next section. A methodological consideration when time-locking person-coded behavior to neural responses is the temporal dimension in which behavior and neural synchrony is assessed. In the case of fNIRS, it takes about 2–4 s for hemodynamic response to initiate (Scholkmann et al., 2014). Hence, we advise careful consideration of the time frame in which behavior is observed and coded, and then time-locked to a hemodynamic response. Electrophysiological responses are elicited much quicker than hemodynamic responses, in milliseconds rather than seconds (Bell, 2020), making time-locking behavior to brain responses a bit easier depending on the behavior of interest being assessed. However, we still recommend informed decisions about the timing-locking of observed behavior with EEG responses. Active social interactions require that individuals continuously and mutually adapt to changes in each other's behavior, rending the time-locking of brain and behavior a serious methodological consideration, regardless of the neuroimaging technique used.

5 A New Approach to the Coupling of Brain and Behavior: Phase Patterning and Direction

An alternative to behavior- and epoch-locked approaches to the coupling of brain and behavior is to compare two sets of time-series data, one obtained from each modality. For example, one could compare coordinated changes in movement data, identified using an automated coding technique like motion energy analysis, with coordinated changes in neural signals obtained through fNIRS hyperscanning in the same participants.

The challenge lies in comparing phase patterning and direction observed in movement data with that obtained from hyperscanning data. Neural and movement data occur at different frequencies, and the rate at which brain signals and movement signals change also differs. This makes it difficult to align changes in one modality with those in another. In Section 2.2.4, we discussed analytic approaches for identifying phase patterning and direction in movement time-series data. In Section 3.1.3, we discussed the potential for applying a similar approach to fNIRS data. What we lack is a method for comparing coordinated changes in the signals obtained from brain and movement data in the same group of participants.

As a step toward addressing this gap in the literature, we recently developed a MATLAB-based toolbox that facilitates phase analysis in wavelet transform coherence, enabling more precise classification of inter-brain synchrony (Gvirts et al., 2023). Conventionally, in the hyperscanning literature, researchers utilizing wavelet transform coherence treated anti-phase interactions similarly to in-phase interactions and overlooked lagged synchrony. Our toolbox differentiates between these synchronization patterns. Specifically, it identifies in-phase synchronization (simultaneous neural activation), lagged synchronization (one brain leading the other), and anti-phase synchronization (one brain increases activity while the other decreases). Such distinctions are critical when considering the types of interactions in which infants and adults typically engage during naturalistic social interactions. For example, neural alignment that occurs with minor temporal delays may indicate a contingent response, whereas in-phase patterns may indicate mirroring.

Theoretically, the tool-box developed for analysis of fNIRS hyperscanning data could also be applied to movement data collected using an automated approach. We present a proof-of-concept study here to demonstrate, first, that our toolbox can be used in both response domains (brain and behavior). Then we tested the validity of this approach by showing the extent to which neural and behavioral data exhibit similar patterns of signal coupling as a function of task demands. Finally, we sought to identify the extent to which these patterns are related to the quality of the dyadic interaction (as measured by maternal sensitivity and dyadic reciprocity), which would be a step toward validating this approach

5.1 Proof-of-Concept Study

5.1.1 Rationale

In the adult literature, a distinction has been made between interpersonal synchrony that arises during regular everyday social interactions (Sylos-Labini et al., 2018), and interpersonal synchrony that emerges intentionally as part of an explicit goal to synchronize movements with another person (Reddish et al., 2013). Automated coding techniques, when applied to adult populations, are sensitive to the differences between these two patterns of movement synchronization (Fujiwara & Yokomitsu, 2021). In addition, these two types of synchrony engage different cognitive and social processes and dissociate in psychopathological populations (Dahan et al., 2020; Fitzpatrick et al., 2016; Granner-Shuman et al., 2021; Marton-Alper et al., 2020). This suggests that they may be mediated by different neural mechanisms (Gvirts et al., 2021; Marton-Alper et al., 2023).

Based on this reasoning, we assessed infant-mother movement and brain synchrony during two tasks: a free play task and an instructed synchronization task. In both tasks, the dyad was presented with a basket of toys. In the free play task mothers were invited to play with their infant as they would at home. In the instructed synchronization task mothers were explicitly instructed to synchronize with their infant. We focused on two patterns of synchronization: in-phase and anti-phase. In-phase synchronization is when members of the dyad exhibit their signal peak at the same point in time, whereas anti-phase synchronization is when members of the dyad exhibit this peak at opposite points in time (Figure 4).

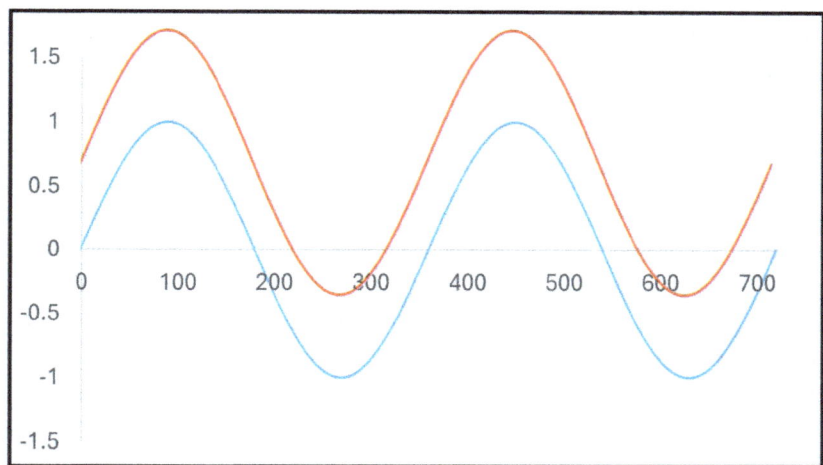

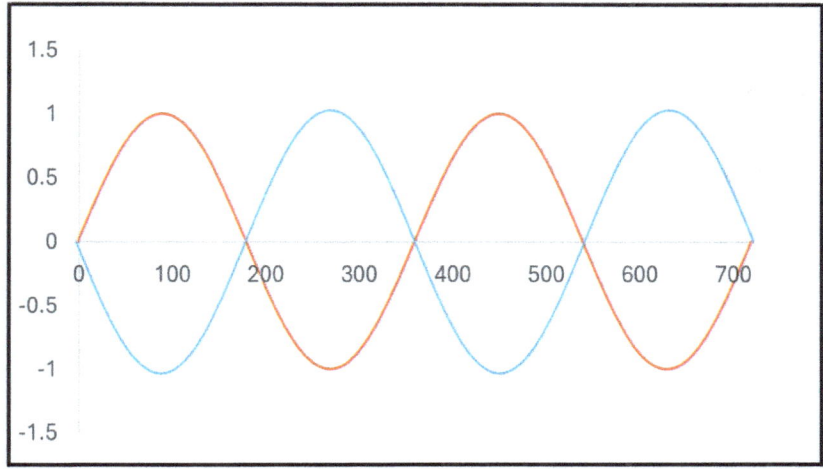

Figure 4 A schematic demonstrating synchrony in-phase and anti-phase patterns using simple sine waves.

5.1.2 Hypotheses

Our first set of hypotheses focused on the type of phase patterning we expected to observe in the two tasks. During free play, one member of the dyad often initiates an exchange, and the other responds in turn (Feldman, 2007). We predicted that this back-and-forth exchange, known as turn-taking, would manifest as anti-phase movement patterns in both the hyperscanning and motion energy analysis data. In contrast, during an instructed synchronization task, where the mother's goal was to synchronize with her infant, we expected the mother to move simultaneously with her infant, mirroring the infant's behavior. We predicted that this behavior would manifest as in-phase movement patterns.

Our second set of hypotheses focused on the relationship between the time-series data obtained from the two modalities. We predicted that the two tasks would elicit distinct patterns of synchronization, which would be observed in both the neural and movement data.

Our third set of hypotheses predicted that phase pattern and direction would be differentially associated with qualitative assessments of the infant-parent interaction. We previously reported that infant-mother movement synchrony, as measured by motion energy analysis and averaged over the course of a free play interaction, was significantly and positively associated with maternal sensitivity and dyadic reciprocity, as assessed by the Coding Interactive Behavior scale (Hammack et al., 2023). These findings revealed that motion energy analysis captures meaningful representations of the infant-parent relationship. Based on these findings, we predicted that during free play, measures of maternal sensitivity and behavioral synchrony (dyadic reciprocity) would be positively associated with the dyad's anti-phase patterning in both the movement and neural data. In contrast, maternal sensitivity and behavioral synchrony would be negatively associated with in-phase patterning, as the mother's goal of synchronizing her behavior with her infant's behavior would override the propensity to respond in a turn-taking, reciprocal fashion. We expected this to be observed in both the movement and neural data.

5.1.3 Experimental Design and Methods

Participants. Ten infants (female = 7) aged 7 to 23 months (M = 14.3 months, SD = 6.3) and their mothers (aged 29 to 48 years, M = 35.2 years, SD = 6.0) were included. The infants were born healthy and full-term with no reported pre- or post-perinatal medical complications and were typically developing. Mothers were White/Non-Hispanic (60%) or White/Hispanic (40%), and all were college educated. All mothers gave informed consent prior to the test session, as approved by the university ethics committee (Florida Atlantic University IRB #1574313).

Procedure. Infant-mother dyads participated in two tasks, each 5 minutes in duration, in this order: (1) a free play task, in which mothers were provided with a small basket of toys and instructed by an experimenter to "play just as you normally would at home," and (2) an instructed synchronization task, in which mothers were provided with a different basket of toys and instructed to "synchronize your behavior with your baby's behavior, whatever that may mean to you." Dyads were seated at a table, with infants in an infant seat to their mother's left (Figure 1, right panel). The test session was video-taped from two camera angles (landscape and overhead) that captured both the infant and mother. Prior to testing, infant and mother were fitted with fNIRS caps set with identical probe geometries (Figure 5). A NIRScout (NIRx Medical Technologies, LLC) was used to acquire the optical imaging data using two wavelengths: 760 nm, which is more sensitive to deoxyhemoglobin (HBR), and 850 nm, which is more sensitive to oxyhemoglobin (HBO).

Treatment and Analysis of Neural and Movement Data. Pre-processing and analysis of the fNIRS data was identical to that reported in Gvirts et al. (2023). Briefly, the optical density data for each member of the dyad were corrected for motion artifacts using wavelet correction, the signals were converted to optical density concentration, and a wavelet transform coherence analysis performed. Next, the LeaderFollowerByPhase Toolbox was used to classify the obtained phase angle values and calculate the percent of time that infant-parent neural signals were observed to be in-phase and anti-phase. More information about the toolbox and how phase angles were classified, and how percentages were calculated, can be found in Gvirts et al. (2023). For simplicity, our analysis focuses on data obtained at channel 18. This channel lies over the temporal

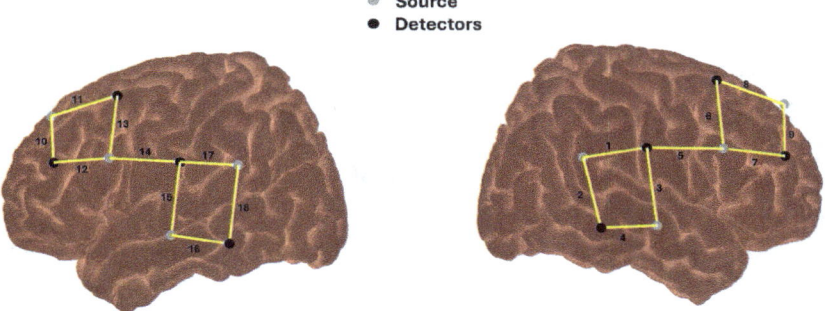

Figure 5 FNIRS probe geometry configuration used in the proof-of-concept study.

parietal junction, an area implicated in neural synchrony in child-parent dyadic interactions (Nguyen, Schleihauf, Kayhan et al., 2021).

The movement data were extracted from the video stream using motion energy analysis (Ramseyer & Tschacher, 2008, 2011) in a manner similar to that described by Hammack et al., (2023). Briefly, using the video data captured by the landscape view, Regions of interest were manually drawn around the members of each video independently to maximize the number of relevant pixels (e.g., the pixels that makeup each member of the dyad). Using motion energy analysis software (Ramseyer & Tschacher, 2008, 2011) the video stream was converted to gray scale and changes in pixel values in the defined regions of interest (Figure 1, right panel) were tabulated. To allow time for the infant and mother to become comfortable in the task, the first minute of the 5-minute task was cropped so that only 4 minutes of dyad interaction was included in the analyses. Two continuous time series were created (one for each dyad member) measuring the amount of body movement of each participant by identifying absolute changes in grayscale values in the regions of interest. The time-series data were then subjected to the LeaderFollowerByPhase Toolbox reported in Gvirts et al. (2023). The toolbox was used to identify phase angles and calculate percent of time that infant-parent dyads were observed to be in-phase and anti-phase, similar to fNIRS data. This process was completed for the free play and the instructed synchronization task, separately.

Qualitative Coding of Infant-Parent Interactions. The Coding Interactive Behavior (CIB) scale (Feldman, 1998) was used to code behavioral measures of parental sensitivity and dyadic reciprocity (i.e., behavioral synchrony) from the recorded sessions of the free play and the instructed synchronization task. Trained coders watched the 4-minute session of each task and manually scored each of the 44 CIB subscales from 1 (minimal amount of the behavior observed) to 5 (a large amount of the behavior observed). Composite scores were then calculated by averaging the relevant subscales for each construct, parental sensitivity, and dyadic reciprocity, resulting in a score between 1 and 5 for each composite. Parental sensitivity is a composite score that was calculated by averaging the following sub scores: acknowledging of infant cues, imitating (in the first year only), elaborating, parent gaze/ joint attention, positive affect, vocal appropriateness, appropriate range of affect, resourcefulness, praising, affectionate touch, and parent supportive presence. Dyadic reciprocity is a composite score that was calculated by averaging the following sub scores: dyadic reciprocity (mutual turn-taking), adaptation-regulation, and fluency. The primary coder was trained directly by Dr. Feldman. Secondary coders were trained by the primary coder on a series of 13 training videos provided by the developer. All coders met at least 80% intercoder reliability on the training videos prior to coding the project data. Coders were blind to the condition at the time of coding, and coders only viewed one condition type per mother-infant dyad. Intercoder reliability was calculated as percent agreement for each task and composite, separately. For free play, 80% of videos were reliability coded; maternal sensitivity reliability = 97.7% and dyadic reciprocity reliability = 91.7%. For instructed synchronization, 100% of videos were reliability coded; maternal sensitivity reliability = 90.3% and dyadic reciprocity reliability = 92.6%.

5.1.4 Data Analysis and Results

The coherence obtained in channel 18 of the fNIRS time-series data and the coherence between the two movement signals were classified according to the LeaderFollowerbyPhase toolbox, respectively. We then calculated the relative amounts (%) of time spent in in-phase and anti-phase coherence for both the fNIRS and movement data separately.

To test the first set of hypothesis – that the free play task would be more likely to elicit anti-phase patterning and the instructed synchronization task would be more likely to elicit in-phase patterning – we compared the relative amount (%) of time spent in in-phase and anti-phase patterning during the free play task versus the instructed synchronization task. To test the second set of hypotheses – that the pattern of results would be observed in both the neural and movement data – analyses were conducted for the hyperscanning and movement data, independently.

For the hyperscanning data, paired sample t-tests (two-tailed) revealed that the mean percentage of time infant-mother dyads spent in anti-phase patterning was significantly greater during the free play task (M = 33.7, SD = 14.4) than during the instructed synchronization task (M = 17.5, SD = 10.0), $t(9) = 2.4$, $p = 0.038$, $d = 0.77$. Conversely, the mean percentage of time spent in in-phase patterning was significantly greater during the instructed synchronization task (M = 27.7, SD = 9.4) than during the free play task (M = 17.4, SD = 7.1), $t(9) = -3.1$, $p = 0.012$, $d = 0.99$. See Figure 6.

For the movement data, the percentage of time spent in anti-phase patterning was significantly greater during the free play task (M = 26.5, SD = 6.4) than during the instructed synchronization task (M = 13.1, SD = 5.5), $t(9) = 4.8$, $p < 0.001$, $d = 1.5$. In contrast, the percentage of time spent in in-phase patterning was significantly greater during the instructed synchronization task (M = 40.3, SD = 14.1) than during the free play task (M = 27.2, SD = 5.2), $t(9) = -3.5$, $p = 0.014$, $d = 1.1$. See Figure 6.

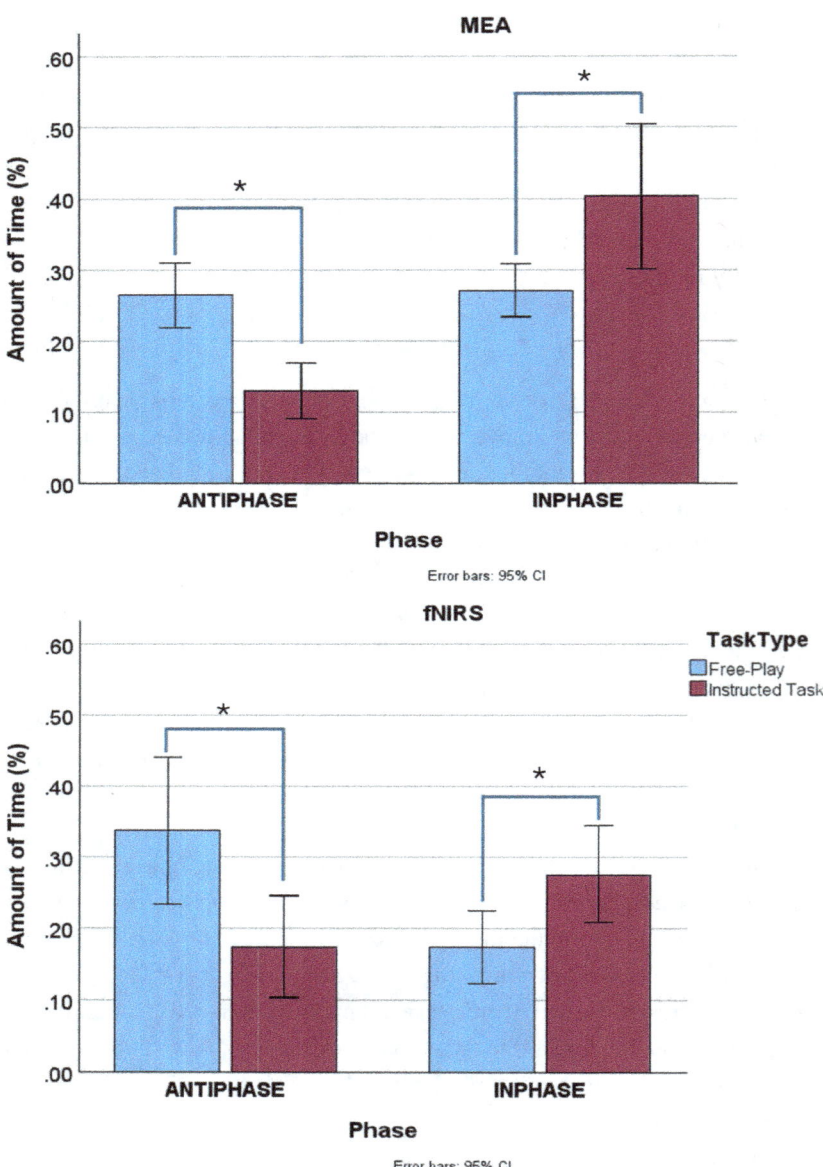

Figure 6 The mean percentage of time dyads spent in anti-phase and in-phase patterning, as observed in the motion energy analysis (MEA) and fNIRS data, during the free play and instructed synchronization task. * p < .05, two-tailed tests.

To test the third set of hypotheses – that phase patterning would be differentially associated with qualitative assessments of the infant-parent interaction – we assessed the relation between phase patterning and CIB codes. Analyses were conducted for neural and movement data, separately.

For the fNIRS hyperscanning data during the free play task, dyadic reciprocity was positively and significantly correlated with anti-phase patterning ($r = 0.655$, $p = 0.040$, 95% CI [0.063 0.906]). Maternal sensitivity was also positively correlated with anti-patterning, although this finding did not reach significance ($r = 0.622$, $p = 0.055$, 95% CI [0.008 0.895]). In contrast, during the instructed synchronization task, dyadic reciprocity ($r = -.888$, $p < 0.001$, 95% CI [-.973 -.582]) and maternal sensitivity ($r = -.809$, $p = 0.005$, 95% CI [-0.952 -0.370]) were negatively and significantly correlated with in-phase patterns. See Figure 7A.

For the movement synchrony data, during the free play task, maternal sensitivity ($r = 0.633$, $p = 0.037$, 95% CI [0.075 0.909]) was positively and significantly correlated with anti-phase patterns. Dyadic reciprocity ($r = 0.304$, $p = 0.393$, 95% CI [-0.372, 0.769]) was not significantly correlated with anti-phase patterns. During the instructed play task, no significant correlations were found between dyadic reciprocity ($r = -0.377$, $p = 0.283$, 95% CI [-0.802, 0.302]) or maternal sensitivity ($r = -0.043$, $p = 0.907$, 95% CI [-0.627, 0.573]) and in-phase patterns. See Figure 7B.

5.1.5 Single Dyad Illustrations

To explore whether task-related differences in phase patterning can be observed at the dyad level, we present two dyads from the sample reported earlier (Figures 8A and 8B). The figure for each dyad includes data obtained during the free play and instructed synchronization task. The percentage of time spent in anti-phase and in-phase patterns, by task, is reported. Also included in the figures are lead-lag patterns (mother-led and infant-led). The LeaderFollowerByPhase Toolbox used for data extraction in this proof-of-concept study calculates the distribution of time across all four phase patterns (Gvirts et al., 2023). Although we focus here only on in-phase and anti-phase patterning, the other phase patterns are included in Figures 8A and 8B.

In the group results, the clearest task-related results were obtained with the fNIRS data. During the free play task, both dyads spent a greater percentage of time in anti-phase than in-phase patterns (Dyad A 32% vs 23% and Dyad B 32% vs 12%). Conversely, during the instructed synchronization task, both dyads spent a greater percentage of time in in-phase than anti-phase patterns, although

A

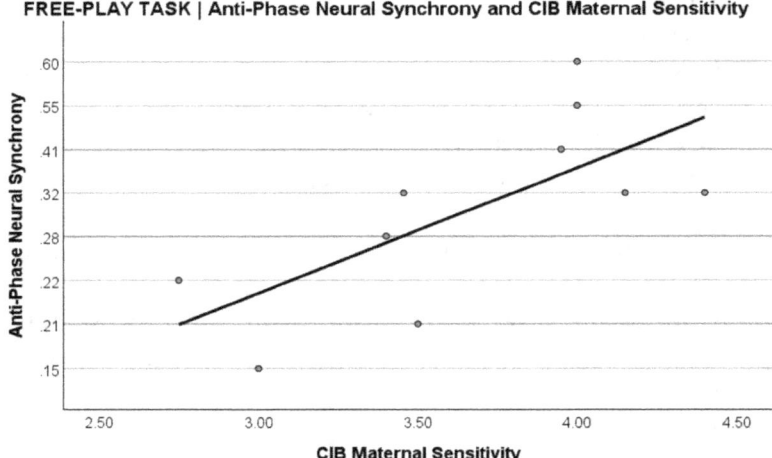

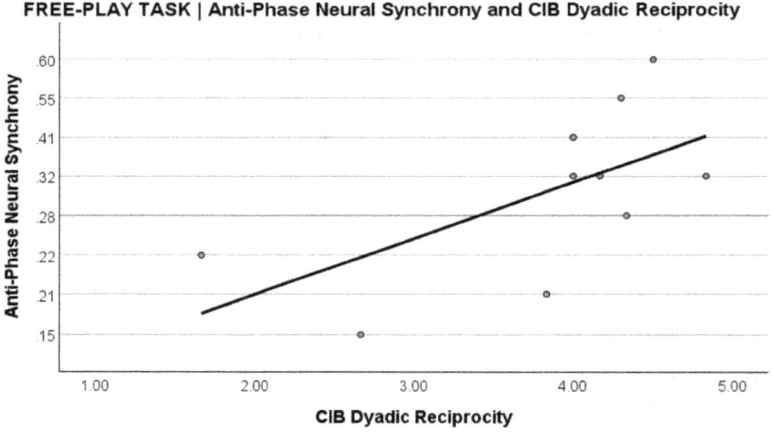

Figure 7A Scatterplots of the correlations obtained between anti-phase patterning and maternal sensitivity (top) and anti-phase patterning and dyadic reciprocity (bottom) during the free play task. Maternal sensitivity and dyadic reciprocity as measured by the Coding Interactive Behavior (CIB) rating system.

the differentiation was greater in Dyad A than Dyad B (Dyad A 33% vs 9% and Dyad B 33% vs 29%).

Task-differentiation was not as clear in the movement data. During the free play task, both dyads spent the same percentage of time in anti-phase and in-phase patterns (Dyad A 27% vs 27% and Dyad B 21% vs 21%). During the instructed synchronization task, both dyads spent a greater percentage of time in in-phase than anti-phase patterns (Dyad A 64% vs 4% and Dyad B 27% vs 20%).

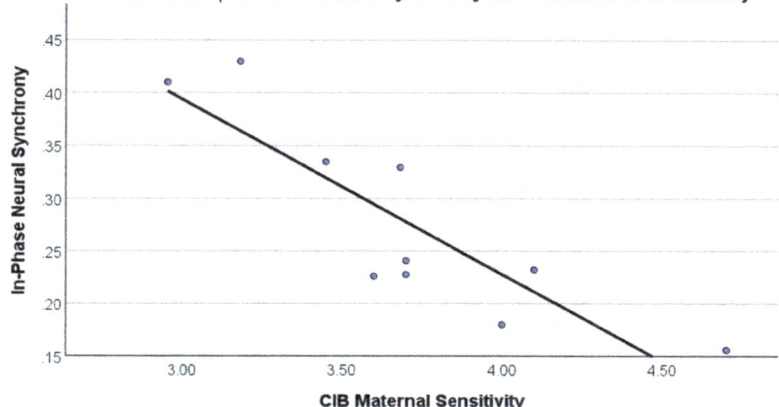

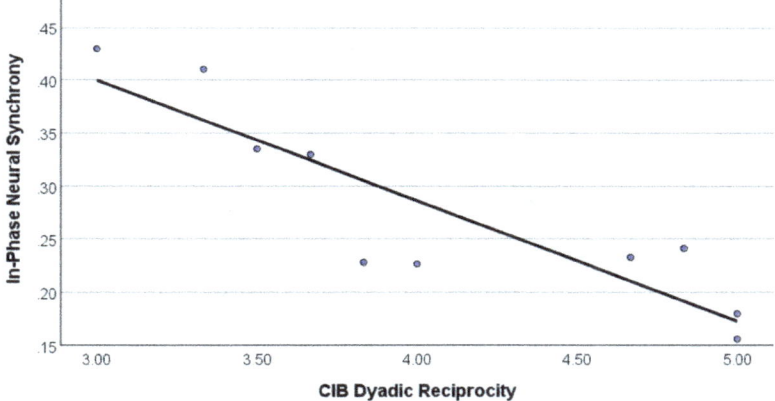

Figure 7B Scatterplots of the correlations obtained between in-phase patterning and maternal sensitivity (top) and in-phase patterning and dyadic reciprocity (bottom), observed in the instructed synchronization task. Maternal sensitivy and dyadic reciprocity as measured by the Coding Interactive Behavior (CIB) rating system.

Together, the group- and individual-level results demonstrate the added value of extracting phase patterning from time-series data. These results also show that access to data from multiple modalities can provide greater insight into our understanding of early emerging infant-parent dyadic interactions.

5.1.6 Discussion

Comparison of the time spent in in-phase and anti-phase patterning revealed a similar pattern of results in the fNIRS and movement synchrony data.

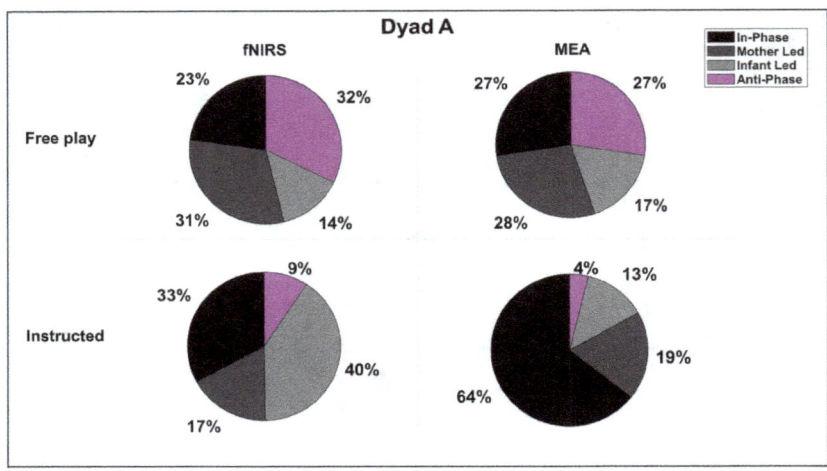

Figure 8A Time percentage pie charts depict how time is distributed across four different phase patterns (in-phase, anti-phase, mother-led, infant-led) during the free play and instructed synchronization tasks for Dyad A

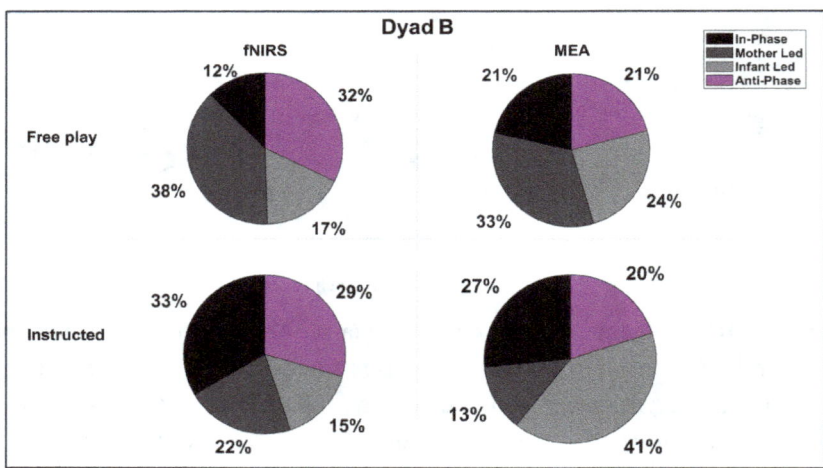

Figure 8B Time percentage pie charts depict how time is distributed across four different phase patterns (in-phase, anti-phase, mother-led, infant-led) during the free play and instructed synchronization tasks for Dyad B.

Infant-mother dyads spent a greater percentage of time in anti-phase patterning during free play than during instructed synchronization, which was observed in both the neural and movement synchrony data. Conversely, infant-mother dyads spent a greater percentage of time in in-phase patterning during instructed synchronization than during free play. These outcomes provide initial support for our hypothesis that different social contexts elicit different interaction patterns and, for the first time, reveal that differential phase patterning can be observed in both fNIRS and movement time-series data.

Examination of the relation between patterns of synchrony and dyadic qualities revealed a clear pattern of results in the hyperscanning data. During the free play task, dyads with mothers who showed greater sensitivity and who engaged in more dyadic reciprocity spent more time in anti-phase patterns, suggesting more turn-taking interactions. In contrast, during the instructed synchronization task, success in moving simultaneously with the infant, perhaps through mirroring, was associated with a decrease in maternal sensitivity and dyadic reciprocity. These outcomes demonstrate that the quality of dyadic interactions is associated with different interaction styles, as reflected in the fNIRS time-series data.

The correlations conducted with the movement synchrony data and dyadic qualities did not yield as clear results as observed in the fNIRS data. For the movement synchrony data, during the free play task, maternal sensitivity was positively and significantly correlated with anti-phase patterns. In contrast, dyadic reciprocity was not significantly correlated with anti-phase patterns. During the instructed play task, no significant correlations were found between dyadic reciprocity or maternal sensitivity and in-phase patterns. It is possible that with a larger sample size, and greater power, significant correlations would be obtained.

Finally, the two single-dyad illustrations revealed that the patterns observed in the group data were also evident at the single-dyad level, including greater task differentiation in the fNIRS than the movement data.

One might wonder why movement synchrony patterning was not as closely associated with maternal sensitivity and dyadic synchrony as neural synchrony patterning. One possibility is that movement energy analysis is a less sensitive measure of synchrony patterning than fNIRS. However, this seems unlikely, given that the phase patterning results for movement energy analysis were similar to those for fNIRS (Figure 6), with both measures differentiating between tasks with similar effect sizes.

Another possibility relates to frame removal when computing movement synchrony. In movement energy analysis, when the boundaries of defined regions of interest overlap, correspondence in movement (measured by changes in grayscale values) cannot be computed. Therefore, frames in the video stream where regions of interest overlapped are removed from the analysis. In the free play and instructed synchronization tasks reported here, the mean (standard deviation) percentage of frames removed from analyses were 21.0% (12.5) and 18.8% (11.4), respectively. This is lower than what has been observed in other studies using online data collection techniques with infant-parent dyads (e.g., Hammack et al., 2023 reported M = 26.8%, SD = 11.1), but still higher than optimal. The loss of data points during the time series may lead to less robust results in some types of analysis.

5.2 Considerations for Future Research

One of the primary advantages of an automated approach is that it provides a means with which to compare, over the course of an interaction, phase patterns in movement synchrony with those observed in neural synchrony. Our proof-of-concept study established that different phase patterns, representing different types of interaction patterns can be observed in both hyperscanning and movement data. In addition, the extent to which these patterns are observed, and their association with qualitative measures of the infant-parent relationship, depends on the context in which the infant-parent interaction takes place.

Our long-term goal is to develop techniques for conducting more detailed analysis of the time-series data, to identify the extent to which changes in brain and behavior occur concurrently or are lagged. Analyses involving time-series data which involve the coupling of brain and behavior require that the neural and the behavioral signals are time locked. There are a number of ways this can be accomplished. For example, post-experiment a stimulus marker can be inserted manually in the neural and behavioral time series to mark the start of the session and relevant points in the time series. Other options are to insert stimulus markers using a manual key press or use automatic forms of triggering during the test session. Techniques that include person-executed marking of the data stream have the potential to be less precise, whereas automatic triggering could be more precise as well as more efficient.

An important consideration in the application of automated coding in conjunction with fNIRS data is sampling rate. Often, neural signals and behavioral signals are collected at different sampling rates. Up sampling or down sampling of the signals will be required to conduct a comparison of changes in the signals over time. When choosing a sampling rate, it is important to consider the frequency with which one expects the signal to change in a meaningful way. For example, meaningful changes in the hemodynamic response occur at a frequency around 0.1 HZ (Scholkmann et al., 2014). In contrast, meaningful changes in movement data range in occurrence depending on the speed of the interaction, generally occurring at a frequency below 4 HZ (and more commonly, between 0.5 and 1.5 HZ) (Fujiwara & Daibo, 2016; Fujiwara & Yokomitsu, 2021). The sample rate used needs to both be compatible with the phenomenon being measured and with the tools used to measure that phenomenon.

Finally, the proof-of-concept study introduces phase angle to the analyses of fNIRS and movement data in the developmental sciences. What is still missing is information about directionality of influence; the causal relation between two signals. The integration of Granger causality analysis, an analytic technique that can shed light on the causal relation between two signals, along with our toolbox, could further enrich the field's understanding of brain-behavior interactions.

6 Conclusions

The study of interpersonal synchrony in the developmental sciences is rapidly expanding. With advancements in automated behavioral coding and fNIRS technology, along with new analytic methods for interpreting brain and behavioral signals, we have unparalleled opportunities to delve into the intricate and diverse interactions between infants and parents. These interactions occur in a wide variety of interpersonal contexts, serve multiple purposes, and are closely linked to linguistic, social, and cognitive outcomes (Feldman et al., 1996; Golds et al., 2022; Kellerman et al., 2020).

Critically, we now have tools to study the temporal dynamics of coordinated changes in brain and behavior during early emerging infant-parent interactions. Traditionally, dyadic interpersonal synchrony has been reported as a single score averaged over portions, or all, of an interactive session. However, dyadic synchrony is dynamic and bidirectional, built through mutual regulatory processes, and involves partners moving into and between coordinated states. What has been slow to emerge in the field are investigations of moment-to-moment changes in interpersonal synchrony that are shaped by both infant and parent, and how these are related to other social constructs. In this Element we introduced analytic techniques that allow us to assess the way in which coordinated movement patterns and interbrain synchrony change over the course of an interaction. These analytic techniques can help identify nuances in patterns of interaction that to date have been overlooked. For example, our proof-of-concept study revealed that different tasks elicited different phase patterns in infant-mother dyads. Anti-phase patterns were more frequently observed during free play, whereas in-phase patterns were more frequently observed during instructed synchronization, in both fNIRS and movement data. The association between phase patterning and maternal sensitivity and dyadic reciprocity also differed by task. Together, these data demonstrate the feasibility, and value, of investigating synchrony as a dynamic construct in both brain and behavior. One challenge, however, is how to link changes in brain to changes in behavior.

6.1 Interpreting Coordinated Changes in Brain and Behavior

As a historical note, initial reports of interbrain synchrony were met with both enthusiasm and words of caution. One primary concern was whether neural synchrony was an epiphenomenon. Perhaps the coordinated changes in brain signals observed were simply a result of two individuals engaged in the same activity simultaneously or could be attributed to shared exposure to low-level environment stimuli, and not indicative of more complex social processes (Hamilton, 2021). These concerns have been greatly reduced by implementation of better research designs, the use of pseudo dyads as controls, and the development of more sophisticated analytic techniques that allow for stronger conclusions to be drawn when interpreting coordinated changes in neural signals. Also alleviating concerns about how to interpret synchronized neural signals is a growing body of research demonstrating a relation between coordinated changes in brain signals and synchrony-related behaviors. Researchers have identified coordinated changes in neural signals that are associated with task demands, are time-locked to the onset of behaviors that facilitate social exchange and are observed selectively in social processing cortical networks. Hence, we have strong evidence that neural synchrony is not incidental but reflects social processing and engagement.

What remains more elusive, however, is how to characterize the relation between coordinated changes in behavioral synchrony, like that observed in movement data, and coordinated changes in neural synchrony, like that observed in fNIRS data. Drawing causal conclusions about the relation between changes in brain activity and changes in behavior is challenging, for two reasons. First, interpersonal synchrony is a complex phenomenon that involves interrelated processes, such as joint attention, shared affect, and common goals. Engagement in these processes is reflected not in a single behavior but a set of behaviors. In addition, dyadic synchrony is supported by not a single brain structure, but a social processing network composed of interacting brain areas. We are just beginning to piece together cognitive-social processes, behaviors, and brain regions activated.

Second, behavioral and cortical activity occur at different frequencies, and change on different time scales. As discussed in Section 5.2, direct comparison of movement and neural time-series data can be challenging. One approach is to down-sample or up-sample the data streams, to be of the same frequency. The sample rate used needs to both be compatible with the phenomenon being measured and with the tools used to measure that phenomenon. An alternative is to apply a window-lagged approach using very brief intervals, preserving the ability to look at changes over the course of an interaction. For instance, one could identify phase values for short time windows (e.g., 3 sec) and use vector autoregressive models to identify the extent to which past phase values of neural synchrony predict future phase values of movement synchrony, or the reverse. One could also include in the analysis other factors, such as maternal sensitivity or infant initiative, that are hypothesized to influence coordinated patterns of neural or behavioral synchrony. Finally, there are models outside the scope of this Element that could be explored, such as mixed-frequency models, machine learning, and hierarchical time-series models, if the approaches we have covered here do not suffice for the hypotheses being tested. Whatever approach is taken, the outcome of work along these lines has the potential to transform our understanding of infant-parent interactions, measured across modalities, tasks, and time.

6.2 Is Interpersonal Synchrony a Developmental Mechanism?

There is a robust body of research showing that behavioral measures of interpersonal synchrony in infant-parent dyads predict cognitive, social, and communicative outcome measures in childhood and adolescence (Feldman, 2012). There is also a growing body of research suggesting a positive association between neural synchrony and developmental outcomes (Bi et al., 2023). Bio-behavior models have been proposed to explain and predict how regulation of brain and behavior during dyadic interactions leads to these positive outcomes, and dysregulation leads to maladaptive outcomes (Feldman, 2007). One might even suggest that brain and behavioral synchrony are developmental mechanisms.

However, we also know that behavioral and neural synchrony alone does not predict outcomes. For example, social support, maternal mental health, and parental stress all influence behavioral and neural measures of infant-parent synchrony (Feldman et al., 2004; Golds et al., 2022; Lundy, 2003). Many of the same factors are associated with, and often predict, social and cognitive functioning in childhood (Feldman et al., 2009). Models that test direct and indirect effects of these factors on measures of interpersonal synchrony and outcome measures are needed before firm conclusions can be drawn about the role that interpersonal personal plays as a developmental mechanism.

We anticipate that specific types of synchronies are linked to distinct outcomes. For instance, coordinated activity between two brains in the prefrontal cortex, associated with ostensive cues, is likely to be a better predictor of language outcomes than coordinated patterns of neural activation in the prefrontal cortex related to affect regulation. The ability to precisely identify connections between brain activity, behavior, and social, cognitive, and communicative outcomes will be crucial.

Finally, much remains to be discovered about the optimal conditions for neural and behavioral synchrony in learning and development. Although it is often assumed that more synchrony is better, there may be an optimal range for positive outcomes, with very high and very low levels of interpersonal synchrony leading to poor outcomes (Roche et al., 2025). Additionally, the flexibility with which dyads transition through and between more or less synchronized states may be a better indicator of healthy social interactions and a stronger predictor of outcomes than the magnitude of synchrony observed (Mayo & Gordon, 2020). In this Element we argue that viewing synchrony as a unidimensional construct measured only by the magnitude of associations between infant and parent, overlooks important nuances in social interaction patterns. Analyzing phase patterns extracted from time-series data, for example, allows us to identify leaders and followers, how this may change over the course of an interaction, and how it is associated with the quality of the interactions. A phase patterning approach also facilitates the exploration of how frequently and flexibly infant-parent dyads move from one phase pattern to another.

6.3 Clinical Applications

New insights into the temporal dynamics of infant-parent synchrony will have wide-ranging implications for clinical applications. The ability to identify disruptions or deficits in infant-parent synchrony may serve as a valuable marker for identifying infants at risk for poor development outcomes. These findings can also offer new avenues for early detection and intervention.

The degree of interpersonal synchrony observed in infant-parent and child-parent dyads has been linked to risk conditions, including parental stress, prematurity, maternal depression and anxiety, and sociodemographics, emphasizing its relevance to developmental psychopathology (Azhari, Bizzego, & Esposito, 2022; Feldman et al., 2004; Hoyniak et al., 2021; Quinoñes-Camacho et al., 2022). Neural imaging work has also revealed that the degree of neural synchrony observed in infant-parent and child-parent dyads might be a biomarker for potential clinical disorders, such as autism spectrum disorder (Wan et al., 2019). To date, developmental studies have focused on the magnitude of synchrony observed as the primary measure of brain and behavioral interpersonal synchrony. Studies that link specific types behavioral and neural synchrony (e.g., in phase, anti-phase) with problematic developmental outcomes will allow greater precision with which to identify infants at risk.

A more complete understanding of how coordinated changes in brain and behavior are related to developmental outcomes will also benefit the design of intervention strategies. Identification of sequences of behavior that are atypical can help clinicians design effective interventions (Morgan et al., 2023; Quinoñes-Camacho et al., 2022). For example, if poorly synchronized infant-parent interactions lack turn-taking episodes and/or infants fail to respond contingently to affective cues, interventions can target these behaviors.

Finally, the development of automated approaches to the coding of dyadic interactions would have the potential to significantly improve access to a wider and diverse population of infants at risk. Despite the critical role of early social interactions in an infant's developmental trajectory, current assessment methods are inadequate, particularly for infants at risk for ASD and attention-deficit/hyperactivity disorder (ADHD). Most tools require complex, time-consuming clinical scoring and fail to capture nuances of social synchronization. The design of a user-friendly, computer-based tool that automatically analyzes video recordings of infant-mother interactions would enable both in-person and remote administration without the complexities of traditional clinical scoring. Early identification of social synchronization issues will enable timely interventions, improving developmental outcomes and address a critical gap in early childhood assessments.

References

Abbasi, H., Mollet, S. R., Williams, S. A. et al. (2023). Deep-learning for automated markerless tracking of infants' general movements. International Journal of Information Technology, 15(8), 4073–4083. https://doi.org/10.1007/s41870-023-01497-z.

Abney, D. H., daSilva, E. B., & Bertenthal, B. I. (2021). Associations between infant–mother physiological synchrony and 4-and 6-month-old infants' emotion regulation. Developmental Psychobiology, 63(6), e22161. https://doi.org/10.1002/dev.22161.

Airaksinen, M., Gallen, A., Kivi, A. et al. (2022). Intelligent wearable allows out-of-the-lab tracking of developing motor abilities in infants. Communications Medicine, 2(1), 69, 1–14. https://doi.org/10.1038/s43856-022-00131-6.

Airaksinen, M., Räsänen, O., Ilén, E. et al. (2020). Automatic posture and movement tracking of infants with wearable movement sensors. Scientific Reports, 10(1), 169. https://doi.org/10.1038/s41598-019-56862-5.

Aksan, N., Kochanska, G., & Ortmann, M. R. (2006). Mutually responsive orientation between parents and their young children: Toward methodological advances in the science of relationships. Developmental Psychology, 42(5), 833–848. https://doi.org/10.1037/0012-1649.42.5.833.

Alghowinem, S., Chen, H., Breazeal, C., & Park, H. W. (2021, December). Body gesture and head movement analyses in dyadic parent-child interaction as indicators of relationship. In 2021 16th IEEE International Conference on Automatic Face and Gesture Recognition (FG 2021), 1–5. https://doi.org/10.1109/FG52635.2021.9666983.

Altmann, U. (2011). Investigation of movement synchrony using windowed cross-lagged regression. In Analysis of Verbal and Nonverbal Communication and Enactment. The Processing Issues: COST 2102 International Conference, Budapest, Hungary, September 7–10, 2010, Revised Selected Papers (pp. 335-345). Springer Berlin Heidelberg. https://doi.org/10.1007/978-3-642-25775-9_31.

Atzil, S., Hendler, T., & Feldman, R. (2014). The brain basis of social synchrony. Social Cognitive and Affective Neuroscience, 9(8), 1193–1202. https://doi.org/10.1093/scan/nst105.

Azhari, A., Bizzego, A., Balagtas, J. P. M., Leng, K. S. H., & Esposito, G. (2022). Asymmetric prefrontal cortex activation associated with mutual gaze of mothers and children during shared play. Symmetry, 14(5), 998. https://doi.org/10.3390/sym14050998.

Azhari, A., Bizzego, A., & Esposito, G. (2021). Father-child dyads exhibit unique inter-subject synchronization during co-viewing of animation video stimuli. Social Neuroscience, 16(5), 522–533. https://doi.org/10.1080/17470919.2021.1970016.

Azhari, A., Bizzego, A., & Esposito, G. (2022). Parent–child dyads with greater parenting stress exhibit less synchrony in posterior areas and more synchrony in frontal areas of the prefrontal cortex during shared play. Social Neuroscience, 17(6), 520–531. https://doi.org/10.1080/17470919.2022.2162118.

Azhari, A., Leck, W. Q., Gabrieli, G. et al. (2019). Parenting stress undermines mother-child brain-to-brain synchrony: A hyperscanning study. Scientific Reports, 9(1), 11407. https://doi.org/10.21979/N9/CTR0YX.

Balconi, M., & Vanutelli, M. E. (2018). Functional EEG connectivity during competition. BMC Neuroscience, 19(1), 63. https://doi.org/10.1186/s12868-018-0464-6.

Barreto, C., Bruneri, G. D. A., Brockington, G., Ayaz, H., & Sato, J. R. (2021). A new statistical approach for fNIRS hyperscanning to predict brain activity of preschoolers' using teacher's. Frontiers in Human Neuroscience, 15, 622146. https://doi.org/10.3389/fnhum.2021.622146.

Bell, M. A. (2020). Mother-child behavioral and physiological synchrony. Advances in Child Development and Behavior, 58, 163–188. Elsevier. https://doi.org/10.1016/bs.acdb.2020.01.006.

Bente, G., & Novotny, E. (2020). Bodies and minds in sync: Forms and functions of interpersonal synchrony in human interaction. In The Handbook of Communication Science and Biology (pp. 416–428). Routledge.

Bernieri, F. J., Reznick, J. S., & Rosenthal, R. (1988). Synchrony, pseudosynchrony, and dissynchrony: Measuring the entrainment process in mother-infant interactions. Journal of Personality and Social Psychology, 54(2), 243–253 https://doi.org/10.1037/0022-3514.54.2.243.

Bertenthal, B. I., & Clifton, R. K. (1998). Perception and action. In W. Damon (Ed.), Handbook of Child Psychology: Vol. 2. Cognition, Perception, and Language (pp. 51–102). John Wiley & Sons.

Bevilacqua, D., Davidesco, I., Wan, L. et al. (2019). Brain-to-brain synchrony and learning outcomes vary by student–teacher dynamics: Evidence from a real-world classroom electroencephalography study. Journal of Cognitive Neuroscience, 31(3), 401–411. https://doi.org/10.1162/jocn_a_01274.

References

Bi, X., Cui, H., & Ma, Y. (2023). Hyperscanning Studies on Interbrain Synchrony and Child Development: A Narrative Review. Neuroscience, 530, 38–45. https://doi.org/j.neuroscence.2023.08.035.

Bizzego, A., Azhari, A., & Esposito, G. (2022). Assessing computational methods to quantify mother-child brain synchrony in naturalistic settings based on fNIRS signals. Neuroinformatics, 20(2), 427–436. https://doi.org/10.1007/s12021-021-09558-z.

Bizzego, A., Battisti, A., Gabrieli, G., Esposito, G., & Furlanello, C. (2019). pyphysio: A physiological signal processing library for data science approaches in physiology. SoftwareX, 10, https://doi.org/10.1016/j.softx.2019.100287.

Boas, D. A., Dale, A. M., & Franceschini, M. A. (2004). Diffuse optical imaging of brain activation: Approaches to optimizing image sensitivity, resolution, and accuracy. NeuroImage, 23, S275–S288. https://doi.org/10.1016/j.neuroimage.2004.07.011.

Cao, Z., Hidalgo, G., Simon, T., Wei, S.-E., & Sheikh, Y. (2021). OpenPose: Realtime multi-person 2D pose estimation using part affinity fields. IEEE Transactions on Pattern Analysis and Machine Intelligence, 43(1), 172–186. https://doi.org/10.1109/TPAMI.2019.2929257.

Chen, M., Minn Chow, S., Hammal, Z., Messinger, D. S., & Cohn, J. F. (2020). A person- and time-varying vector autoregressive model to capture interactive infant-mother head movement dynamics. Multivariate Behavioral Research, 56(5), 739–767. https://doi.org/10.1080/00273171.2020.1762065.

Coburn, S. S., Crnic, K. A., & Ross, E. K. (2015). Mother–infant dyadic state behaviour: Dynamic systems in the context of risk. Infant and Child Development, 24(3), 274–297. https://doi.org/10.1002/icd.1913.

Cornejo, C., Cuadros, Z., Morales, R., & Paredes, J. (2017). Interpersonal coordination: Methods, achievements, and challenges. Frontiers in Psychology, 8, 1685. https://doi.org/10.3389/fpsyg.2017.01685.

Cuadros, Z., Carré, D., Hurtado, E., & Cornejo, C. (2021). Interpersonal coordination in three- year-old children: Functions, morphology, and temporality. Acta Psychologica, 218, 103351. https://doi.org/10.1016/j.actpsy.2021.103351.

Cuadros, Z., Hurtado, E., & Cornejo, C. (2019). Measuring dynamics of infant-adult synchrony through mocap. Frontiers in Psychology, 10, 2839. https://doi.org/10.3389/fpsyg.2019.02839.

Cuadros, Z., Hurtado, E., & Cornejo, C. (2020). Infant-adult synchrony in spontaneous and nonspontaneous interactions. PLOS ONE, 15(12), e0244138. https://doi.org/10.1371/journal.pone.0244138.

Cui, X., Bryant, D. M., & Reiss, A. L. (2012). NIRS-based hyperscanning reveals increased interpersonal coherence in superior frontal cortex during cooperation. NeuroImage, 59(3), 2430–2437. https://doi.org/10.1016/j.neuroimage.2011.09.003.

Czeszumski, A., Eustergerling, S., Lang, A. et al. (2020). Hyperscanning: A Valid method to study neural inter-brain underpinnings of social interaction. Frontiers in Human Neuroscience, 14, 1–17. https://doi.org/10.3389/fnhum.2020.00039.

Dahan, A., Dubnov, Y. A., Popkov, A. Y., Gutman, I., & Probolovski, H. G. (2020). Brief report: Classification of autistic traits according to brain activity recorded by fNIRS using ε-complexity coefficients. Journal of Autism and Developmental Disorders, 1–11. https://doi.org/10.1007/s10803-020-04793-w.

Datavyu Team (2014). Datavyu: A video coding tool. Databrary Project, New York University. http://datavyu.org.

Davis, M., Bilms, J., & Suveg, C. (2017). In sync and in control: A meta-analysis of parent–child positive behavioral synchrony and youth self-regulation. Family Process, 56(4), 962–980. https://doi.org/10.1111/famp.12259.

Davis, M., West, K., Bilms, J., Morelen, D., & Suveg, C. (2018). A systematic review of parent–child synchrony: It is more than skin deep. Developmental Psychobiology, 60(6), 674–691. https://doi.org/10.1002/dev.21743.

de Graag, J. A., Cox, R. F., Hasselman, F., Jansen, J., & de Weerth, C. (2012). Functioning within a relationship: Mother–infant synchrony and infant sleep. Infant Behavior and Development, 35(2), 252–263. https://doi.org/10.1016/j.infbeh.2011.12.006.

Deater-Deckard, K., Pylas, M. V., & Petrill, S. A. (1997). The Parent-Child Interaction System (PARCHISY). London: Institute of Psychiatry.

Decety, J., Jackson, P. L., Sommerville, J. A., Chaminade, T., & Meltzoff, A. N. (2004). The neural bases of cooperation and competition: An fMRI investigation. NeuroImage, 23(2), 744–751. https://doi.org/10.1016/j.neuroimage.2004.05.025.

DePasquale, C. E. (2020). A systematic review of caregiver–child physiological synchrony across systems: Associations with behavior and child functioning. Development and Psychopathology, 32(5), 1754–1777. https://doi.org/10.1017/S0954579420001236.

Doba, K., Pezard, L., & Nandrino, J. L. (2022). How do maternal emotional regulation difficulties modulate the mother–infant behavioral synchrony? Infancy, 27(3), 582–608. https://doi.org/10.1111/infa.12461.

Duan, H., Yang, T., Wang, X. et al. (2022). Is the creativity of lovers better? A behavioral and functional near-infrared spectroscopy hyperscanning study.

Current Psychology, 41(1), 41–54. https://doi.org/10.1007/s12144-020-01093-5.

Dunbar, N. E., Burgoon, J. K., & Fujiwara, K. (2022). Automated methods to examine nonverbal synchrony in dyads. Proceedings of Machine Learning Research, 173, 204–217.

Egmose, I., Varni, G., Cordes, K. et al. (2017). Relations between automatically extracted motion features and the quality of mother-infant interactions at 4 and 13 months. Frontiers in Psychology, 8, 2178. https://doi.org/10.3389/fpsyg.2017.02178.

Emberson, L. L., Zinszer, B. D., Raizada, R. D., & Aslin, R. N. (2017). Decoding the infant mind: Multivariate pattern analysis (MVPA) using fNIRS. PloS ONE, 12(4), https://doi.org/10.1371/journal.pone.0172500.

Erel, Y., Jaffe-Dax, S., Yeshurun, Y., & Bermano, A. H. (preprint). STORM-Net : Simple and timely optode registration method for functional near-infrared spectroscopy (fNIRS). bioRxiv, 12.29.424683. https://doi.org/10.1101/2020.12.29.424683.

Fang, H., Li, J., Tang, H. et al. (2022). AlphaPose: Whole-body regional multi-person pose estimation and tracking in real-time. IEEE Transactions on Pattern Analysis and Machine Intelligence, 45(6), 7157–7173. https://doi.org/10.1109/TPAMI.2022.3222784.

Feldman, R. (1998). Coding interactive behavior manual. Unpublished Manual; Bar-Ilan University, Israel.

Feldman, R. (2003). Infant–mother and infant–father synchrony: The coregulation of positive arousal. Infant Mental Health Journal: Official Publication of the World Association for Infant Mental Health, 24(1), 1–23. https://doi.org/10.1002/imhj.10041.

Feldman, R. (2006). From biological rhythms to social rhythms: Physiological precursors of mother-infant synchrony. Developmental Psychology, 42(1), 175–188. https://doi.org/10.1037/0012-1649.42.1.175.

Feldman, R. (2007). Parent–infant synchrony and the construction of shared timing; physiological precursors, developmental outcomes, and risk conditions. Journal of Child psychology and Psychiatry, 48(3–4), 329–354. https://doi.org/10.1111/j.1469-7610.2006.01701.x.

Feldman, R. (2012). Parent-infant synchrony: A biobehavioral model of mutual influences in the formation of affiliative bonds. Monographs of the Society for Research in Child Development, 77(2), 42–51. https://doi.org/10.1111/j.1540-5834.2011.00600.x.

Feldman, R., & Eidelman, A. I. (2004). Parent-infant synchrony and the social-emotional development of triplets. Developmental Psychology, 40(6), 1133.

Feldman, R., Eidelman, A. I., & Rotenberg, N. (2004). Parenting stress, infant emotion regulation, maternal sensitivity, and the cognitive development of triplets: A model for parent and child influences in a unique ecology. Child Development, 75(6), 1774–1791.

Feldman, R., Granat, A. D. I., Pariente, C. et al. (2009). Maternal depression and anxiety across the postpartum year and infant social engagement, fear regulation, and stress reactivity. Journal of the American Academy of Child & Adolescent Psychiatry, 48(9), 919–927.

Feldman, R., & Greenbaum, C. W. (1997). Affect regulation and synchrony in mother – infant play as precursors to the development of symbolic competence. Infant Mental Health Journal, 18(1), 4–23. https://doi.org/10.1002/(SICI)1097-0355(199721)18:1<4::AID-IMHJ2>3.0.CO;2-R.

Feldman, R., Greenbaum, C. W., Yirmiya, N., & Mayes, L. C. (1996). Relations between cyclicity and regulation in mother-infant interaction at 3 and 9 months and cognition at 2 years. Journal of Applied Developmental Psychology, 17(3), 347–365. https://doi.org/10.1016/S0193-3973(96)90031-3.

Feldman, R., Magori-Cohen, R., Galili, G., Singer, M., & Louzoun, Y. (2011). Mother and infant coordinate heart rhythms through episodes of interaction synchrony. Infant Behavior and Development, 34(4), 569–577. https://doi.org/10.1016/j.infbeh.2011.06.008.

Field, T., Healy, B., & LeBlanc, W. G. (1989). Sharing and synchrony of behavior states and heart rate in nondepressed versus depressed mother-infant interactions. Infant Behavior and Development, 12(3), 357–376. https://doi.org/10.1016/0163-6383(89)90044-1.

Filippetti, M. L., Andreu-Perez, J., De Klerk, C., Richmond, C., & Rigato, S. (2023). Are advanced methods necessary to improve infant fNIRS data analysis? An assessment of baseline-corrected averaging, general linear model (GLM) and multivariate pattern analysis (MVPA) based approaches. NeuroImage, 265, 119756. https://doi.org/10.1016/j.neuroimage.2022.119756.

Fitzpatrick, P., Frazier, J. A., Cochran, D. M. et al. (2016). Impairments of social motor synchrony evident in autism spectrum disorder. Frontiers in Psychology, 7. https://doi.org/10.3389/fpsyg.2016.01323.

Franchak, J. M., Tang, M., Rousey, H., & Luo, C. (2024). Long-form recording of infant body position in the home using wearable inertial sensors. Behavior Research Methods, 56, 4982–5001. https://doi.org/10.3758/s13428-023-02236-9.

Friston, K. J. (1994). Functional and effective connectivity in neuroimaging: A synthesis. Human Brain Mapping, 2(1–2), 56–78. https://doi.org/10.1002/hbm.460020107.

Fujiwara, K., & Daibo, I. (2016). Evaluating interpersonal synchrony: Wavelet transform toward an unstructured conversation. Frontiers in Psychology, 7, 516. https://doi.org/10.3389/fpsyg.2016.00516.

Fujiwara, K., Kimura, M., & Daibo, I. (2020). Rhythmic features of movement synchrony for bonding individuals in dyadic interaction. Journal of Nonverbal Behavior, 44(1), 173–193. https://doi.org/10.1007/s10919-019-00315-0.

Fujiwara, K., & Yokomitsu, K. (2021). Video-based tracking approach for nonverbal synchrony: A comparison of Motion Energy Analysis and OpenPose. Behavior Research Methods, 53(6), 2700–2711. https://doi.org/10.3758/s13428-021-01612-7.

Funamoto, A., & Rinaldi, C. M. (2015). Measuring parent–child mutuality: A review of current observational coding systems. Infant Mental Health Journal, 36(1), 3–11. https://doi.org/10.1002/imhj.21481.

Fusaroli, R., Konvalinka, I., & Wallot, S. (2014). Analyzing social interactions: The promises and challenges of using cross recurrence quantification analysis. In Translational Recurrences: From Mathematical Theory to Real-World Applications (pp. 137–155). Cham: Springer International.

Gemignani, J., de la Cruz-Pavía, I., Martinez, A. et al. (2023). Reproducibility of infant fNIRS studies: A meta-analytic approach. Neurophotonics, 10(2), 023518.

Gemignani, J., & Gervain, J. (2021). Comparing different pre-processing routines for infant fNIRS data. Developmental Cognitive Neuroscience, 48, 100943. https://doi.org/10.1016/j.dcn.2021.100943.

Golds, L., Gillespie-Smith, K., Nimbley, E., & MacBeth, A. (2022). What factors influence dyadic synchrony? A systematic review of the literature on predictors of mother–infant dyadic processes of shared behavior and affect. Infant Mental Health Journal, 43(5), 808–830. https://doi.org/10.1002/imhj.22011.

Gordon, I., & Feldman, R. (2008). Synchrony in the triad: A microlevel process model of coparenting and parent-child interactions. Family Process, 47(4), 465–479. https://doi.org/10.1111/j.1545-5300.2008.00266.x.

Gordon, I., Zagoory-Sharon, O., Leckman, J. F., & Feldman, R. (2010). Prolactin, oxytocin, and the development of paternal behavior across the first six months of fatherhood. Hormones and Behavior, 58(3), 513–518. https://doi.org/10.1016/j.yhbeh.2010.04.007.

Granger, C. W. J. (1969). Investigating causal relations by econometric models and cross-spectral methods. Econometrica, 37(3), 424. https://doi.org/10.2307/1912791.

Granner-Shuman, M., Dahan, A., Yozevitch, R., & Problovski, H. Z. G. (2021). The association among autistic traits, interactional synchrony and typical pattern of motor planning and execution in neurotypical individuals. Symmetry, 13(6), 1034. https://doi.org/10.3390/SYM13061034.

Gratier, M. (2003). Expressive timing and interactional synchrony between mothers and infants: Cultural similarities, cultural differences, and the immigration experience. Cognitive Development, 18(4), 533–554.

Grossmann, T., & Johnson, M. H. (2010). Selective prefrontal cortex responses to joint attention in early infancy. Biology Letters, 6(4), 540–543. http://dx.doi.org/10.1098/rsbl. 2009.1069.

Grossmann, T., Parise, E., & Friederici, A. D. (2010). The detection of communicative signals directed at the self in infant prefrontal cortex. Frontiers in Human Neuroscience, 4, 201. http://dx.doi.org/10.3389/fnhum.2010.00201.

Gvirts Probolovski, H. Z. (2020). Commentary: Using second-person neuroscience to elucidate the mechanisms of reciprocal social interaction. Frontiers in Behavioral Neuroscience, 14, 13.

Gvirts Problovski, H. Z., Lavi, D., Yozevitch, R. et al. (2021). Impairments of interpersonal synchrony evident in attention deficit hyperactivity disorder (ADHD). Acta Psychologica, 212, 103210. https://doi.org/10.1016/j.actpsy.2020.103210.

Gvirts, H. Z., & Perlmutter, R. (2020). What guides us to neurally and behaviorally align with anyone specific? A neurobiological model based on fNIRS hyperscanning studies. The Neuroscientist, 26(2), 108–116.

Gvirts Provolovski, H. Z., Sharma, M., Gutman, I. et al. (2023). New framework for understanding cross-brain coherence in functional near-infrared spectroscopy (fNIRS) hyperscanning studies. Journal of Visualized Experiments, (200), e65347. https://doi.org/10.3791/65347.

Ham, J., & Tronick, E. (2009). Relational psychophysiology: Lessons from mother–infant physiology research on dyadically expanded states of consciousness. Psychotherapy Research, 19(6), 619–632. https://doi.org/10.1080/10503300802609672.

Hamilton, A. F. D. C. (2021). Hyperscanning: Beyond the hype. Neuron, 109(3), 404–407.

Hammack, J., Sharma, M., Riera-Gomez, L., Gvirts, H. Z., & Wilcox, T. (2023). When I move, you move: Associations between automatic and person-coded measures of infant-mother synchrony during free-play using virtual in-home data collection. Infant Behavior and Development, 72, 2. https://doi.org/10.1016/j.infbeh.2023.101869.

Hammal, Z., Cohn, J. C., & Messinger, D. S. (2015). Head movement dynamics during play and perturbed mother-infant interaction. IEEE Transactions on Affective Computing, 6(4), 361–370. 10.1109/TAFFC.2015.2422702.

Harel, H., Gordon, I., Geva, R., & Feldman, R. (2010). Gaze behaviors of preterm and full-term infants in nonsocial and social contexts of increasing dynamics: Visual recognition, attention regulation, and gaze synchrony. Infancy, 16(1), 69–90. https://doi.org/10.1111/j.1532-7078.2010.00037.x.

Haresign, I. M., Phillips, E. A. M., Whitehorn, M., et al. (2022). Measuring the temporal dynamics of inter-personal neural entrainment in continuous child-adult EEG hyperscanning data. Developmental cognitive neuroscience, 54, 101093.

Haufe, S., Nikulin, V. V., Müller, K. R., & Nolte, G. (2013). A critical assessment of connectivity measures for EEG data: A simulation study. NeuroImage, 64, 120–133. https://doi.org/10.1016/j.neuroimage.2012.09.036.

Healey, D. M., Gopin, C. B., Grossman, B. R., Campbell, S. B., & Halperin, J. M. (2010). Mother–child dyadic synchrony is associated with better functioning in hyperactive/inattentive preschool children. Journal of Child Psychology and Psychiatry, 51(9), 1060–1061. https://doi.org/10.1111/j.1469-7610.2010.02220.x.

Hesse, N., Pujades, S., Black, M. J. et al. (2019). Learning and tracking the 3D body shape of freely moving infants from RGB-D sequences. IEEE Transactions on Pattern Analysis and Machine Intelligence, 42(10), 2540–2551. https://doi.org/10.1109/TPAMI.2019.2917908.

Hoch, J. E., Ossmy, O., Cole, W. G., Hasan, S., & Adolph, K. E. (2021). "Dancing" together: Infant–mother locomotor synchrony. Child Development, 92(4), 1337–1353. https://doi.org/10.1111/cdev.13513.

Hoehl, S., & Markova, G. (2018). Moving developmental social neuroscience toward a second-person approach. PLoS Biology, 16(12), e3000055. https://doi.org/10.1371/journal.pbio.3000055.

Hove, M. J., & Risen, J. L. (2009). It's all in the timing: Interpersonal synchrony increases affiliation. Social Cognition, 27(6), 949–960. https://doi.org/10.1521/soco.2009.27.6.949.

Hoyniak, C. P., Quiñones-Camacho, L. E., Camacho, M. C. et al. (2021). Adversity is linked with decreased parent-child behavioral and neural synchrony. Developmental Cognitive Neuroscience, 48, 100937. https://doi.org/10.1016/j.dcn.2021.100937.

Huang, X., Fu, N., Liu, S., & Ostadabbas, S. (2021). Invariant representation learning for infant pose estimation with small data. 2021 16th IEEE International Conference on Automatic Face and Gesture Recognition (FG 2021), 1–8. https://doi.org/10.1109/FG52635.2021.9666956.

Hyde, D. C., Simon, C. E., Ting, F., & Nikolaeva, J. I. (2018). Functional organization for theory of mind in pre-verbal infants: A near-infrared spectroscopy study. The Journal of Neuroscience, 38(18), 4264–4274.

Ilyka, D., Johnson, M. H., & Lloyd-Fox, S. (2021). Infant social interactions and brain development: A systematic review. Neuroscience & Biobehavioral Reviews, 130, 448–469.

Isabella, R. A., & Belsky, J. (1991). Interactional synchrony and the origins of infant-mother attachment: A replication study. Child Development, 62(2), 373–384.

Isabella, R. A., Belsky, J., & von Eye, A. (1989). Origins of infant-mother attachment: An examination of interactional synchrony during the infant's first year. Developmental Psychology, 25(1), 12–21. https://doi.org/10.1037/0012-1649.25.1.12.

Issartel, J., Bardainne, T., Gaillot, P., & Marin, L. (2015). The relevance of the cross-wavelet transform in the analysis of human interaction – A tutorial. Frontiers in Psychology, 5. https://doi.org/10.3389/fpsyg.2014.01566.

Jebeli, A., Chen, L. K., Guerrerio, K. et al. (2024). Quantifying the quality of parent-child interaction through machine-learning based audio and video analysis: Towards a vision of AI-assisted coaching support for social workers. ACM Journal on Computing and Sustainable Societies, 2(1), 1–21. https://doi.org/10.1145/3617693.

Jiang, J., Dai, B., Peng, D. et al. (2012). Neural synchronization during face-to-face communication. Journal of Neuroscience, 32(45), 16064–16069. https://doi.org/10.1523/JNEUROSCI.2926-12.2012.

Kalal, Z., Mikolajczyk, K., & Matas, J. (2012). Tracking-learning-detection. IEEE Transactions on Pattern Analysis and Machine Intelligence, 34, 1409–1422. http://dx.doi.org/10.1109/TPAMI.2011.239.

Karaca, B., Salah, A. A., Denissen, J., Poppe, R., & de Zwarte, S. M. (2024, May). Survey of automated methods for nonverbal behavior analysis in parent-child interactions. In 2024 IEEE 18th International Conference on Automatic Face and Gesture Recognition (FG) (pp. 1–11). https://doi.org/10.1109/FG59268.2024.10582009.

Karger, R. H. (1979). Synchrony in mother-infant interactions. Child Development, 50(3), 882–885. https://doi.org/10.2307/1128959.

Keefe, M. R., Kotzer, A. M., Froese-Fretz, A., & Curtin, M. (1996). A longitudinal comparison of irritable and nonirritable infants. Nursing Research, 45(1), 4–9. https://doi.org/10.1097/00006199-199601000-00002.

Kellerman, A. M., Schwichtenberg, A. J., Abu-Zhaya, R. et al. (2020). Dyadic synchrony and responsiveness in the first year: Associations with autism risk. Autism Research, 13(12), 2190–2201. https://doi.org/10.1002/aur.2373.

Klein, L., Ardulov, V., Hu, Y. et al. (2020, October). Incorporating measures of intermodal coordination in automated analysis of infant-mother interaction. In Proceedings of the 2020 International Conference on Multimodal Interaction (pp. 287–295). https://doi.org/10.1145/3382507.3418870.

Koehne, S., Hatri, A., Cacioppo, J. T., & Dziobek, I. (2016). Perceived interpersonal synchrony increases empathy: Insights from autism spectrum disorder. Cognition, 146, 8–15. https://doi.org/10.1016/j.cognition.2015.09.007.

Leclère, C., Avril, M., Viaux-Savelon, S. et al. (2016). Interaction and behaviour imaging: A novel method to measure mother–infant interaction using video 3D reconstruction. Translational Psychiatry, 6(5), e816. https://doi.org/10.1038/tp.2016.82.

Leclère, C., Viaux, S., Avril, M. et al. (2014). Why synchrony matters during mother-child interactions: A systematic review. PloS ONE, 9(12), e113571. https://doi.org/10.1371/journal.pone.0113571.

Lemus, A., Vogel, S. C., Greaves, A. N., & Brito, N. H. (2022). Maternal anxiety symptoms associated with increased behavioral synchrony in the early postnatal period. Infancy, 27(4), 821–835. https://doi.org/10.1111/infa.12473.

Leo, M., Bernava, G. M., Carcagnì, P., & Distante, C. (2022). Video-based automatic baby motion analysis for early neurological disorder diagnosis: State of the art and future directions. Sensors, 22(3), 866. https://doi.org/10.3390/s22030866.

Leong, V., Byrne, E., Clackson, K. et al. (2017). Speaker gaze increases information coupling between infant and adult brains. Proceedings of the National Academy of Sciences, 114(50), 13290–13295. https://doi.org/10.1073/pnas.1702493114.

Li, Y., Halleck, T. Q., Evans, L. et al. (2024). Eye of the beholder: Neural synchrony of dynamically changing relations between parent praise and child affect. Developmental Science, 27(6), e13541. https://doi.org/10.1111/desc.13541.

Liu, S., Han, Z. R., Xu, J. et al. (2024). Parenting links to parent–child interbrain synchrony: A real-time fNIRS hyperscanning study. Cerebral Cortex, 34(2), bhad533. https://doi.org/10.1093/cercor/bhad533.

Liu, Y., Moss, E., Ting, F., & Hyde, D. C. (2025). Neural sensitivity to others' belief states in infancy predicts later theory of mind reasoning in childhood. Cortex, 184, 96–105. https://doi.org/10.1016/j.cortex.2024.11.023.

Liu, J., Zhang, R., Geng, B. et al. (2019). Interplay between prior knowledge and communication mode on teaching effectiveness: Interpersonal neural synchronization as a neural marker. NeuroImage, 193, 93–102. https://doi.org/10.1016/j.neuroimage.2019.03.004.

Liu, Q., Zhu, S., Zhou, X. et al. (2024). Mothers and fathers show different neural synchrony with their children during shared experiences. NeuroImage, 288, 120529.

Lloyd-Fox, S., Richards, J. E., Blasi, A. et al. (2014). Coregistering functional near-infrared spectroscopy with underlying cortical areas in infants. Neurophotonics, 1(20), 025006. https://doi.org/10.1117/1.NPh.1.2.025006.

Longhi, E. (2009). "Songese": Maternal structuring of musical interaction with infants. Psychology of Music, 37(2), 195–213. https://doi.org/10.1177/0305735608097042.

López Pérez, D., Leonardi, G., Niedźwiecka, A. et al. (2017). Combining recurrence analysis and automatic movement extraction from video recordings to study behavioral coupling in face-to-face parent-child interactions. Frontiers in Psychology, 8, 2228. https://doi.org/10.3389/fpsyg.2017.02228.

Lotzin, A., Romer, G., Schiborr, J. et al. (2015). Gaze synchrony between mothers with mood disorders and their infants: Maternal emotion dysregulation matters. PLoS ONE, 10(12), e0144417. https://doi.org/10.1371/journal.pone.0144417.

Loulis, S., & Kuczynski, L. (1997). Beyond one hand clapping: Seeing bidirectionality in parent-child relations. Journal of Social and Personal Relationships, 14(4), 441–461. https://doi.org/10.1177/0265407597144002.

Lourenço, V., Coutinho, J., & Pereira, A. F. (2021). Advances in microanalysis: Magnifying the social microscope on mother-infant interactions. Infant Behavior and Development, 64, 101571. https://doi.org/10.1016/j.infbeh.2021.101571.

Lu, K., Qiao, X., Yun, Q., & Hao, N. (2021). Educational diversity and group creativity: Evidence from fNIRS hyperscanning. NeuroImage, 243, 118564. https://doi.org/https://doi.org/10.1016/j.neuroimage.2021.118564.

Lu, K., Xue, H., Nozawa, T., & Hao, N. (2019). Cooperation makes a group be more creative. Cerebral Cortex, 29(8), 3457–3470. https://doi.org/10.1093/cercor/bhy215.

Lundy, B. L. (2003). Father–and mother–infant face-to-face interactions: Differences in mind-related comments and infant attachment? Infant Behavior and Development, 26(2), 200–212.

MacLean, P. C., Rynes, K. N., Aragón, C. et al. (2014). Mother–infant mutual eye gaze supports emotion regulation in infancy during the still-face paradigm. Infant Behavior and Development, 37(4), 512–522. https://doi.org/10.1016/j.infbeh.2014.06.008.

Marriott Haresign, I., Phillips, E. A. M., & Wass, S. V. (2024). Why behaviour matters: Studying inter-brain coordination during child-caregiver interaction.

Developmental Cognitive Neuroscience, 67, 101384. https://doi.org/10.1016/j.dcn.2024.101384.

Marriott Haresign, I., Phillips, E. A. M., Whitehorn, M. et al. (2023). Gaze onsets during naturalistic infant-caregiver interaction associate with "sender" but not "receiver" neural responses, and do not lead to changes in inter-brain synchrony. Scientific Reports, 13(1), 3555. https://doi.org/10.1038/s41598-023-28988-0.

Marton-Alper, I. Z., Gvirts-Provolovski, H. Z., Nevat, M., Karklinsky, M., & Shamay-Tsoory, S. G. (2020). Herding in human groups is related to high autistic traits. Scientific Reports, 10(1). https://doi.org/10.1038/s41598-020-74951-8.

Marton-Alper, I. Z., Markus, A., Nevat, M., Bennet, R., & Shamay-Tsoory, S. G. (2023). Differential contribution of between and within-brain coupling to movement synchronization. Human Brain Mapping, 44(10), 4136–4151.

Mathis, A., Mamidanna, P., Cury, K. M. et al. (2018). DeepLabCut: Markerless pose estimation of user-defined body parts with deep learning. Nature Neuroscience, 21, 1281–1289. https://doi.org/10.1038/s41593-018-0209-y.

Mayo, O., & Gordon, I. (2020). In and out of synchrony – Behavioral and physiological dynamics of dyadic interpersonal coordination. Psychophysiology, 57(6), e13574. https://doi.org/10.1111/psyp.13574.

McDonald, N. M., & Perdue, K. L. (2018). The infant brain in the social world: Moving toward interactive social neuroscience with functional near-infrared spectroscopy. Neuroscience & Biobehavioral Reviews, 87, 38–49.

Miller, J. G., Vrtička, P., Cui, X. et al. (2019). Inter-brain synchrony in mother-child dyads during cooperation: An fNIRS hyperscanning study. Neuropsychologia, 124, 117–124. https://doi.org/10.1016/j.neuropsychologia.2018.12.021.

Minagawa, Y., Hata, M., Yamamoto, E., Tsuzuki, D., & Morimoto, S. (2023). Inter-brain synchrony during mother–infant interactive parenting in 3–4-month-old infants with and without an elevated likelihood of autism spectrum disorder. Cerebral Cortex, 33(24), 11609–11622. https://doi.org/10.1093/cercor/bhad395.

Mize, J., & Pettit, G. S. (1997). Mothers' social coaching, mother-child relationship style, and children's peer competence: Is the medium the message? Child Development, 68(2), 312–332. https://doi.org/10.2307/1131852.

Moore, G. A., & Calkins, S. D. (2004). Infants' vagal regulation in the still-face paradigm is related to dyadic coordination of mother-infant interaction. Developmental Psychology, 40(6), 1068. https://doi.org/10.1037/0012-1649.40.6.1068.

References

Moore, G. A., Quigley, K. M., Voegtline, K. M., & DiPietro, J. A. (2016). Don't worry, be (moderately) happy: Mothers' anxiety and positivity during pregnancy independently predict lower mother–infant synchrony. Infant Behavior and Development, 42, 60–68. https://doi.org/10.1016/j.infbeh.2015.11.002.

Morgan, R., Fischer, R., & Bulbulia, J. A. (2017). To be in synchrony or not? A meta-analysis of synchrony's effects on behavior, perception, cognition and affect. Journal of Experimental Social Psychology, 72, 13–20. https://doi.org/10.1016/j.jesp.2017.03.009.

Morgan, J. K., Santosa, H., Conner, K. K. et al. (2023). Mother–child neural synchronization is time linked to mother–child positive affective state matching. Social Cognitive and Affective Neuroscience, 18(1), nsad001.

Nazneen, T., Islam, I. B., Sajal, Md. S. R. et al. (2022). Recent trends in non-invasive neural recording based brain-to-brain synchrony analysis on multidisciplinary human interactions for understanding brain dynamics: A systematic review. Frontiers in Computational Neuroscience, 16, 875282. https://doi.org/10.3389/fncom.2022.875282.

Ngueyep, R., & Serban, N. (2015). Large-vector autoregression for multilayer spatially correlated time series. Technometrics, 57(2), 207–216.

Nguyen, T., Abney, D. H., Salamander, D., Bertenthal, B. I., & Hoehl, S. (2021). Proximity and touch are associated with neural but not physiological synchrony in naturalistic mother-infant interactions. NeuroImage, 244, 118599. https://doi.org/10.1016/j.neuroimage.2021.118599.

Nguyen, T., Hoehl, S., & Vrtička, P. (2021). A guide to parent-child fNIRS hyperscanning data processing and analysis. Sensors, 21(12), 4075. https://doi.org/10.3390/s21124075.

Nguyen, T., Kungl, M. T., Hoehl, S., White, L. O., & Vrtička, P. (2023). Visualizing the invisible tie: Linking parent–child neural synchrony to parents' and children's attachment representations. Developmental Science, e13504. https://doi.org/10.1111/desc.13504.

Nguyen, T., Schleihauf, H., Kayhan, E. et al. (2020). The effects of interaction quality on neural synchrony during mother-child problem solving. Cortex, 124, 235–249. https://doi.org/10.1016/j.cortex.2019.11.020.

Nguyen, T., Schleihauf, H., Kayhan, E. et al. (2021). Neural synchrony in mother–child conversation: Exploring the role of conversation patterns. Social Cognitive and Affective Neuroscience, 16(1–2), 93–102. https://doi.org/10.1093/scan/nsaa079.

Nguyen, T., Schleihauf, H., Kungl, M. et al. (2021). Interpersonal neural synchrony during father–child problem solving: An fNIRS hyperscanning study. Child Development, 92(4), e565–e580. https://doi.org/10.1111/cdev.13510.

Nguyen, T., Zimmer, L., & Hoehl, S. (2023). Your turn, my turn: Neural synchrony in mother–infant proto-conversation. Philosophical Transactions of the Royal Society B, 378(1875), 20210488. https://doi.org/10.1098/rstb.2021.0488.

Oku, A. Y. A., Barreto, C., Bruneri, G. et al. (2022). Applications of graph theory to the analysis of fNIRS data in hyperscanning paradigms. Frontiers in Computational Neuroscience, 16, 975743. https://doi.org/10.3389/fncom.2022.975743.

Owen, M. T., Barfoot, B., Vaughn, A., Domingue, G., & Ware, A. M. (1996). 54-month parent-child structured interaction qualitative rating scales. NICHD Study of Early Child Care Research Consortium: Washington, DC.

Pan, Y., Cheng, X., Zhang, Z., Li, X., & Hu, Y. (2017). Cooperation in lovers: An fNIRS-based hyperscanning study. Human Brain Mapping, 38(2), 831–841. https://doi.org/10.1002/hbm.23421.

Pan, Y., Dikker, S., Goldstein, P. et al. (2020). Instructor-learner brain coupling discriminates between instructional approaches and predicts learning. NeuroImage, 211, 116657. https://doi.org/10.1016/j.neuroimage.2020.116657.

Papoutselou, E., Harrison, S., Mai, G. et al. (2024). Investigating mother–child inter-brain synchrony in a naturalistic paradigm: A functional near infrared spectroscopy (fNIRS) hyperscanning study. European Journal of Neuroscience, 59(6), 1386–1403. https://doi.org/10.1111/ejn.16233.

Perner, J., & Roessler, J. (2012). From infants' to children's appreciation of belief. Trends in Cognitive Sciences, 16(10), 519e525.

Pasiak, C. A. (2017). Elucidating the Effect of Mother-Child Interactional Synchrony: Relations between Synchrony, Mutuality, Parenting Attitudes, and Preschool Adjustment (Doctoral dissertation, University of Windsor (Canada)).

Pasiak, C., & Menna, R. (2015). Mother–child synchrony: Implications for young children's aggression and social competence. Journal of Child and Family Studies, 24(10), 3079–3092. https://doi.org/10.1007/s10826-015-0113-y.

Piazza, E. A., Hasenfratz, L., Hasson, U., & Lew-Williams, C. (2020). Infant and adult brains are coupled to the dynamics of natural communication. Psychological Science, 31(1), 6–17. https://doi.org/10.1177/0956797619878698.

Piazza, E. A., Lordan, M. C., Hasenfratz, L., Hasson, U., & Lew-Williams, C. (2019). Using naturalistic paradigms to study how adult speakers accommodate infant listeners' unique processing demands. The Journal of the Acoustical Society of America, 145(3_Supplement), 1730. https://doi.org/10.1121/1.5101354.

Pouw, W., Trujillo, J. P., & Dixon, J. A. (2020). The quantification of gesture–speech synchrony: A tutorial and validation of multimodal data acquisition using device-based and video-based motion tracking. Behavior Research Methods, 52(2), 723–740. https://doi.org/10.3758/s13428-019-01271-9.

Provenzi, L., Scotto di Minico, G., Giusti, L., Guida, E., & Müller, M. (2018). Disentangling the dyadic dance: Theoretical, methodological and outcomes systematic review of mother-infant dyadic processes. Frontiers in Psychology, 9, 348. https://doi.org/10.3389/fpsyg.2018.00348.

Pukhova, V. M., Kustov, T. V, & Ferrini, G. (2018). Time-frequency analysis of non-stationary signals. 2018 IEEE Conference of Russian Young Researchers in Electrical and Electronic Engineering (EIConRus), 1141–1145. https://doi.org/10.1109/EIConRus.2018.8317292.

Quiñones-Camacho, L. E., Fishburn, F. A., Camacho, M. C., Wakschlag, L. S., & Perlman, S. B. (2019). Cognitive flexibility-related prefrontal activation in preschoolers: A biological approach to temperamental effortful control. Developmental Cognitive Neuroscience, 38, 100651. https://doi.org/10.1016/j.dcn.2019.100651.

Quiñones-Camacho, L. E., Hoyniak, C. P., Wakschlag, L. S., & Perlman, S. B. (2022). Getting in synch: Unpacking the role of parent–child synchrony in the development of internalizing and externalizing behaviors. Development and Psychopathology, 34(5), 1901–1913.

Ramseyer, F. T. (2020). Motion energy analysis (MEA): A primer on the assessment of motion from video. Journal of Counseling Psychology, 67(4), 536–549. https://doi.org/10.1037/cou0000407.

Ramseyer, F., & Tschacher, W. (2008). Synchrony in dyadic psychotherapy sessions. In S. Vrobel, O. E. Rössler, & T. Marks-Tarlow (Eds.), Simultaneity: Temporal Structures and Observer Perspectives, (pp. 329–347). World Scientific. https://doi.org/10.1142/9789812792426_0020.

Ramseyer, F., & Tschacher, W. (2011). Nonverbal synchrony in psychotherapy: Coordinated body movement reflects relationship quality and outcome. Journal of Consulting and Clinical Psychology, 79(3), 284–295. https://doi.org/10.1037/a0023419.

Redcay, E., & Schilbach, L. (2019). Using second-person neuroscience to elucidate the mechanisms of social interaction. Nature Reviews Neuroscience, 20(8), 495–505. https://doi.org/10.1038/s41583-019-0179-4.

Reddish, P., Fischer, R., & Bulbulia, J. (2013). Let's dance together: Synchrony, shared intentionality and cooperation. PLoS ONE, 8(8), e71182. https://doi.org/10.1371/journal.pone.0071182.

Reindl, V., Gerloff, C., Scharke, W., & Konrad, K. (2018). Brain-to-brain synchrony in parent-child dyads and the relationship with emotion regulation revealed by fNIRS-based hyperscanning. NeuroImage, 178, 493–502. https://doi.org/10.1016/j.neuroimage.2018.05.060.

Reindl, V., Konrad, K., Gerloff, C. et al. (2019). Conducting hyperscanning experiments with functional near-infrared spectroscopy. JoVE (Journal of Visualized Experiments), (143), e58807. https://doi.org/10.3791/58807.

Reindl, V., Wass, S., Leong, V. et al. (2022). Multimodal hyperscanning reveals that synchrony of body and mind are distinct in mother-child dyads. NeuroImage, 251, 118982. https://doi.org/10.1016/j.neuroimage.2022.118982.

Reyna, B. A., Brown, L. F., Pickler, R. H., Myers, B. J., & Younger, J. B. (2012). Mother–infant synchrony during infant feeding. Infant Behavior and Development, 35(4), 669–677. https://doi.org/10.1016/j.infbeh.2012.06.003.

Rochat, P., & Goubet, N. (1995). Development of sitting and reaching in 5- to 6-month-old infants. Infant Behavior & Development, 18(1), 53–68. https://doi.org/10.1016/0163-6383(95)90007-1.

Roche, E. C., Redcay, E., & Romeo, R. R. (2025). Caregiver-child neural synchrony: Magic, mirage, or developmental mechanism? Developmental Cognitive Neuroscience, 71, 101482.

Schilbach, L., Timmermans, B., Reddy, V. et al. (2013). Toward a second-person neuroscience. Behavioral and Brain Sciences, 36(4), 393–414. https://doi.org/10.1017/S0140525X12000660.

Schmidt, R. C., & Fitzpatrick, P. (2019). Embodied synchronization and complexity in a verbal interaction. Nonlinear Dynamics, Psychology, and Life Sciences, 23(2), 199–228.

Schmidt, R. C., & Richardson, M. J. (2008). Dynamics of interpersonal coordination. In A. Fuchs & V. K. Jirsa (Eds.), Coordination: Neural, Behavioral and Social Dynamics (pp. 281–308). Berlin, Heidelberg: Springer. https://doi.org/10.1007/978-3-540-74479-5_14.

Schoenherr, D., Paulick, J., Strauss, B. M. et al. (2019). Identification of movement synchrony: Validation of windowed cross-lagged correlation and-regression with peak-picking algorithm. PloS ONE, 14(2), e0211494. https://doi.org/10.1371/journal.pone.0211494.

Scholkmann, F., Kleiser, S., Metz, A. J. et al. (2014). A review on continuous wave functional near-infrared spectroscopy and imaging instrumentation and methodology. NeuroImage, 85(Pt. 1), 6–27. https://doi.org/10.1016/j.neuroimage.2013.05.004.

Shamay-Tsoory, S. G., Saporta, N., Marton-Alper, I. Z, & Gvirts, H. Z (2019). Herding brains: A core neural mechanism for social alignment. Trends in Cognitive Sciences, 23(3), 174–186.

Shin, H. I., Shin, H.-I., Bang, M. S. et al. (2022). Deep learning-based quantitative analyses of spontaneous movements and their association with early neurological development in preterm infants. Scientific Reports, 12(1), 3138. https://doi.org/10.1038/s41598-022-07139-x.

Skuban, E. M., Shaw, D. S., Gardner, F., Supplee, L. H., & Nichols, S. R. (2006). The correlates of dyadic synchrony in high-risk, low-income toddler boys. Infant Behavior and Development, 29(3), 423–434. https://doi.org/10.1016/j.infbeh.2006.02.004.

Soska, K. C., Adolph, K. E., & Johnson, S. P. (2010). Systems in development: Motor skill acquisition facilitates three-dimensional object completion. Developmental Psychology, 46(1), 129–138. https://doi.org/10.1037/a0014618.

Stamate, D., Davuloori, P., Logofatu, D. et al. (2024, June). Ensembles of bidirectional LSTM and GRU neural nets for predicting mother-infant synchrony in videos. In International Conference on Engineering Applications of Neural Networks (pp. 329–342). Cham: Springer Nature. https://doi.org/10.1007/978-3-031-62495-7_25.

Stamate, D., Haran, R., Rutkowska, K. et al. (2023, September). Predicting high vs low mother-baby synchrony with GRU-based ensemble models. In International Conference on Artificial Neural Networks (pp. 191–199). Cham: Springer Nature Switzerland. https://doi.org/10.1007/978-3-031-44201-8_16.

Sun, B., Xiao, W., Feng, X. et al. (2020). Behavioral and brain synchronization differences between expert and novice teachers when collaborating with students. Brain and Cognition, 139, 105513. https://doi.org/https://doi.org/10.1016/j.bandc.2019.105513.

Sylos-Labini, F., d'Avella, A., Lacquaniti, F., & Ivanenko, Y. (2018). Human-human interaction forces and interlimb coordination during side-by-side walking with hand contact. Frontiers in Physiology, 9, 179. https://doi.org/10.3389/fphys.2018.00179.

Tamis-LeMonda, C. S., Ahuja, P., Hannibal, B., Shannon, J., & Spellmann, M. (2002). Caregiver-Child affect, responsiveness, and engagement scale (C-CARES). *Unpublished manuscript.*

Theyer, A., Davidson, C., Amaireh, G., & Wijeakumar, S. (2024). Association between caregiver and infant visual neurocognition. Infant Behavior and Development, 76. https://doi.org/10.1016/j.infbeh.2024.101975.

Thompson, L. A., & Trevathan, W. R. (2009). Cortisol reactivity, maternal sensitivity, and infant preference for mother's familiar face and rhyme in 6-month-old infants. Journal of Reproductive and Infant Psychology, 27(2), 143–167. https://doi.org/10.1080/02646830801918463.

Tronick, E. Z., & Cohn, J. F. (1989). Infant-mother face-to-face interaction: Age and gender differences in coordination and the occurrence of miscoordination. Child Development, 60(1), 85–92. https://doi.org/10.2307/1131074.

Tsai, S.-Y., Barnard, K. E., Lentz, M. J., & Thomas, K. A. (2011). Mother-infant activity synchrony as a correlate of the emergence of circadian rhythm. Biological Research for Nursing, 13(1), 80–88. https://doi.org/10.1177/1099800410378889.

Tsuzuki, D., Jurcak, V., Singh, A. K. et al. (2007). Virtual spatial registration of stand-alone fNIRS data to MNI space. NeuroImage, 34(4), 1506–1518. https://doi.org/10.1016/j.neuroimage.2006.10.043.

Vacharkulksemsuk, T., & Fredrickson, B. L. (2012). Strangers in sync: Achieving embodied rapport through shared movements. Journal of Experimental Social Psychology, 48(1), 399–402. https://doi.org/10.1016/j.jesp.2011.07.015.

Valdesolo, P., Ouyang, J., & DeSteno, D. (2010). The rhythm of joint action: Synchrony promotes cooperative ability. Journal of Experimental Social Psychology, 46(4), 693–695. https://doi.org/10.1016/j.jesp.2010.03.004.

Van Dijk, M., Leonardi, G., Pérez, D. L., & Rączaszek-Leonardi, J. (2022). Co-regulation of movements during infant feeding. Infant Behavior and Development, 69, 101755. https://doi.org/10.1016/j.infbeh.2022.101755.

Vicaria, I. M., & Dickens, L. (2016). Meta-analyses of the intra- and interpersonal outcomes of interpersonal coordination. Journal of Nonverbal Behavior, 40(4), 335–361. https://doi.org/10.1007/s10919-016-0238-8.

Walton, A. E., Richardson, M. J., Langland-Hassan, P., & Chemero, A. (2015). Improvisation and the self-organization of multiple musical bodies. Frontiers in Psychology, 6. https://doi.org/10.3389/fpsyg.2015.00313.

Wan, M. W., Green, J., & Scott, J. (2019). A systematic review of parent–infant interaction in infants at risk of autism. Autism, 23(4), 811–820.

Wass, S. V., Whitehorn, M., Marriott Haresign, I., Phillips, E., & Leong, V. (2020). Interpersonal neural entrainment during early social interaction. Trends in Cognitive Sciences, 24(4), 329–342. https://doi.org/10.1016/j.tics.2020.01.006.

Weinberg, M. K., Tronick, E. Z., Cohn, J. F., & Olson, K. L. (1999). Gender differences in emotional expressivity and self-regulation during early infancy. Developmental Psychology, 35(1), 175. https://doi.org/10.1037//0012-1649.35.1.175.

West, K. L., Zuppichini, M. D., Turner, M. P. et al. (2019). BOLD hemodynamic response function changes significantly with healthy aging. NeuroImage, 188, 198–207. https://doi.org/10.1016/j.neuroimage.2018.12.012.

Xu, T., & Yu, C. (2016). Quantifying joint activities using cross-recurrence block representation. In Proceedings of the Annual Meeting of the Cognitive Science Society (Vol. 38).

Yücel, M. A., Lühmann, A. V., Scholkmann, F. et al. (2021). Best practices for fNIRS publications. Neurophotonics, 8(1), 012101. https://doi.org/10.1117/1.NPh.8.1.012101.

Yurtsever, M., & Eken, S. (2022). BabyPose: Real-time decoding of baby's nonverbal communication using 2D video-based pose estimation. IEEE Sensors Journal, 22(14). https://doi.org/10.1109/JSEN.2022.3183502.

Zhang, W., Qiu, L., Tang, F., & Li, H. (2023). Affective or cognitive interpersonal emotion regulation in couples: An fNIRS hyperscanning study. Cerebral Cortex, 33(12), 7960–7970.

Zhao, H., Li, Y., Wang, X. et al. (2022). Inter-brain neural mechanism underlying turn-based interaction under acute stress in women: A hyperscanning study using functional near-infrared spectroscopy. Social Cognitive and Affective Neuroscience, 17(9), 850–863. https://doi.org/10.1093/scan/nsac005.

Zhu, Y., Leong, V., Hou, Y. et al. (2022). Instructor–learner neural synchronization during elaborated feedback predicts learning transfer. Journal of Educational Psychology, 114(6), 1427–1441. https://doi.org/10.1037/edu0000707.

Cambridge Elements

Research Methods for Developmental Science

Brett Laursen
Florida Atlantic University

Brett Laursen is a Professor of Psychology at Florida Atlantic University. He is Editor-in-Chief of the *International Journal of Behavioral Development,* where he previously served as the founding Editor of the Methods and Measures section. Professor Laursen received his Ph.D. in Child Psychology from the Institute of Child Development at the University of Minnesota and an Honorary Doctorate from Örebro University, Sweden. He is a Docent Professor of Educational Psychology at the University of Helsinki, and a Fellow of the American Psychological Association (Division 7, Developmental), the Association for Psychological Science, and the International Society for the Study of Behavioural Development. Professor Laursen is the co-editor of the *Handbook of Developmental Research Methods* and the *Handbook of Peer Interactions, Relationships, and Groups*.

About the Series

Each offering in this series will focus on methodological innovations and contemporary strategies to assess adjustment and measure change, empowering scholars of developmental science who seek to optimally match their research questions to pioneering methods and quantitative analyses.

Cambridge Elements

Research Methods for Developmental Science

Elements in the Series

Measurement Burst Designs to Improve Precision in Peer Research
Ryan J. Persram, Bianca Panarello, Melisa Castellanos, Lisa Astrologo and William M. Bukowski

Language Assessments for Preschool Children: Validity and Reliability of Two New Instruments Administered by Childcare Educators
Anders Højen, Dorthe Bleses and Philip S. Dale

Parceling in Structural Equation Modeling: A Comprehensive Introduction for Developmental Scientists
Todd D. Little, Charlie Rioux, Omolola A. Odejimi and Zachary L. Stickley

Identifying and Minimizing Measurement Invariance among Intersectional Groups: The Alignment Method Applied to Multi-category Items
Rachel A. Gordon, Tianxiu Wang, Hai Nguyen and Ariel M. Aloe

Algorithms for Measurement Invariance Testing: Contrasts and Connections
Veronica Cole and Conor H. Lacey

Children's Voices and Agency: Ways of Listening in Early Childhood Quantitative, Qualitative and Mixed Methods Research
Jane Spiteri

New Approaches to Assessing Behavioral and Brain Synchrony in Infant-Parent Dyads
Teresa Wilcox, Jacqueline Stotler Hammack, Lindsey Riera-Gomez, Mini Sharma and Hila Gvirts

A full series listing is available at www.cambridge.org/ERMD

For EU product safety concerns, contact us at Calle de José Abascal, 56–1°, 28003 Madrid, Spain or eugpsr@cambridge.org.